BOTÁNICA
Los Angeles

BOTÁNICA *Los Angeles*

Latino Popular Religious Art in the City of Angels

PATRICK ARTHUR POLK

With contributions by

Donald J. Cosentino
Ysamur Flores-Peña
Miki Garcia
Claudia J. Hernández
Michael Owen Jones
Yves Marton

UCLA FOWLER MUSEUM OF CULTURAL HISTORY
LOS ANGELES

Funding for *Botánica Los Angeles: Latino Popular Culture in the City of Angels* has been provided by

The Donald B. Cordry Memorial Fund
Jim and Jeanne Pieper
Monica Salinas
Yvonne Lenart Public Programs Fund
UCLA School of the Arts and Architecture
Manus, the support group of the UCLA
Fowler Museum of Cultural History

Funding for *Infinito Botánica L.A.: A Project by Franco Mondini-Ruiz* has been provided by

Dallas Price-Van Breda
Shirley and Ralph Shapiro

The Fowler Museum is part of
UCLA's School of the Arts and Architecture

Lynne Kostman, *Managing Editor*
Danny Brauer, *Designer and Production Manager*
Don Cole, *Principal Photographer*
David L. Fuller, *Cartographer*

UCLA Fowler Museum of Cultural History
Box 951549, Los Angeles, California 90095-1549

Requests for permission to reproduce material from this volume should be sent to the UCLA Fowler Museum Publications Department at the above address.

Printed and bound in Hong Kong
by South Sea International Press, Ltd.

Library of Congress Cataloging-in-Publication Data

Polk, Patrick Arthur.
    Botánica Los Angeles : Latino popular religious art in the city of angels / Patrick Arthur Polk ; with contributions by Donald J. Cosentino...[et al.].
        p. cm.
    Includes bibliographical references and index.
    ISBN 0-9748729-0-3
    1. Religious articles—California—Los Angeles. 2. Afro-Caribbean cults—California—Los Angeles. 3. Los Angeles (Calif.)—Religious life and customs. I. Cosentino, Donald, 1941–. II. Title.

BL2566.U6P65 2004
299.6'89729'097494—dc22

                    2004048007

CONTENTS

FOREWORD

The exploration of religious systems is a long-standing emphasis of the UCLA Fowler Museum. Within this broad area of inquiry, we have focused particularly upon the ways in which ritual and devotion have been defined and assisted by special categories of objects that vividly illustrate the intertwining of aesthetic choices and religious efficacy. Our investigations have also sought to demonstrate that the line separating the sacred from the secular is not always a distinct one. Spiritual belief and practice in most world cultures are woven tightly into the fabric of daily life, and objects that feed and support such belief systems are as easily situated on a home altar as they are in houses of worship or community shrines.

Botánica Los Angeles: Latino Popular Religious Art in the City of Angels addresses precisely these issues, investigating a highly visible program of vernacular spiritual practice and its expression via a rich array of sculpture and other significant ritual objects and materials. Despite the fact that hundreds of botánicas dot the streets of Los Angeles and its environs, many Angelenos rarely see or notice them. Their "invisibility" may be due to their geographic location or to their unfamiliarity. This publication and the exhibition it accompanies will unfold for our readers and audiences some of the ways in which botánicas function as sites for spiritual advice, alternative healthcare, community building, and distinctive artistic expression—especially for, but certainly not limited to, peoples of Latino descent. For an ever-increasing number of immigrants from Mexico, Central America, and the Caribbean, the botánica has become a potent vehicle for coping with the complexities and challenges of contemporary American life. In this sense *Botánica Los Angeles* resembles other Fowler Museum exhibitions that have sought to demystify misunderstood and unfamiliar vernacular religious practices. It follows in the tradition of the seminal 1995/1996 exhibition *Sacred Arts of*

Haitian Vodou, and two smaller exhibitions, *Santos de Palo: The Household Saints of Puerto Rico* (1994) and *Cuando Hablan Los Santos: Contemporary Santero Traditions from Northern New Mexico* (1997).

———◆◆———

Botánica Los Angeles developed from a long-standing research effort undertaken by several faculty members in UCLA's Department of World Arts and Cultures, all of whom have contributed essays to this publication. Patrick Arthur Polk, visiting assistant professor in the department and its museum scientist, has conducted extensive fieldwork in Los Angeles and has documented and surveyed botánicas since the late 1980s as part of his ongoing research on Afro-Caribbean religions and religious folk art. He estimates that he has visited between two and three hundred botánicas over the years. From 1999 to 2003, Patrick, along with Professors Donald J. Cosentino and Michael Owen Jones, was involved in a collaborative research project investigating botánicas as sites of alternative medical practice. This included interviewing practitioners, documenting their lives and work, and interpreting the ways in which religious imagery has been incorporated into these highly charged sites of healing and worship. This present volume and accompanying exhibition represent the first significant outcomes of this important research effort, with additional publications forthcoming from the other participants. *Botánica Los Angeles* is yet another in a long line of collaborations between the Fowler Museum and UCLA faculty and graduate students. We remain honored to present the results of their fascinating research on traditions as near as our own backyard and as far afield as continental Africa and its Diasporas.

When I assumed the position of director of the Fowler Museum in the fall of 2001, Patrick A. Polk was one of the first of my UCLA colleagues to arrange for a meeting. He shared his pictures of botánicas and virtually bubbled over with enthusiasm for the possibility of an exhibition on this intriguing topic. Patrick had been involved in several previous Fowler projects (*Sequined Spirits: Contemporary Vodou Flags* [1996]; *Cruisin', Stylin', and Pedal Scrapin': The Art of the Lowrider Bicycle* [1998]; and *Muffler Men, Muñecos, and Other Welded Wonders* [1999]) and had consistently translated his original research into lively and accessible exhibitions and publications. The Fowler's exhibition development team was unanimous in its support of his botánicas proposal, and we launched the effort in 2002. We were all aware of the richness and importance of the material and wanted to underscore the relevance of botánicas to an understanding of and appreciation for our own city, its cultural diversity, its artistic inventiveness, and its fast-changing demographics.

Our deepest thanks go to Patrick for his dedication to *Botánica Los Angeles* and for working effectively and diplomatically with a long list of artists, practitioners, and scholars, not to mention the Fowler Museum staff. Throughout this complex project, Patrick's contributions as curator, author, and editor have been superlative. I also applaud his receptivity to presenting as a companion to *Botánica Los Angeles* a site-specific installation by the New York-based artist Franco Mondini-Ruiz, as a part of his *Infinito Botánica* series. This ongoing project—

part sculptural installation and part performance—began in 1996 when Mondini-Ruiz purchased an actual botánica in San Antonio. Mondini-Ruiz's installations are always a dialogue between a controlled modernist grid and a dizzying array of objects. Each is a reinterpretation of the botánica in a contemporary context but always with specific reference to the place in which the installation is produced. For his *Infinito Botánica Los Angeles*, he will concentrate on the fascinating intersections between the botánica—a site of possibility, transformation, and hybridity—and Los Angeles, a sprawling city where a multiplicity of people have come to find fortune and fame and to fulfill their dreams and destinies. In each, as the artist notes, there is the splendor of visual extravaganza but with clearly differing goals and objectives. By pairing the two exhibitions, we hope to give our audiences a chance to explore the collision and collusion of artifice and efficacy. Our warm thanks go to Franco for accepting our invitation and for entering with boundless energy, enthusiasm, and humor into a new conversation between the sacred and the profane.

The Fowler Museum owes a debt of gratitude to the authors who have contributed to this volume: Donald J. Cosentino, Ysamur Flores-Peña, Miki Garcia, Claudia J. Hernández, Michael Owen Jones, and Yves Marton. The diversity of their disciplinary approaches and perspectives has made this volume a ground breaking contribution to the study of vernacular religions, rituals, and arts. Special recognition must again go to Patrick A. Polk, whose two introductory chapters so powerfully familiarize the reader with botánicas and their roles in Los Angeles, as well as with the complex ways the sacred is expressed and invoked via material objects within these establishments. We also thank the many practitioners, healers, and artists who agreed to share their lives and work, as well as re-creating their shrines and altars within the Museum or permitting them to be reproduced here. In many cases the personal has become public, and we are grateful for the willing-ness of the individuals involved to share their deeply held beliefs and processes with us. Many of them have lent objects of devotion to the Museum, and we recognize with gratitude what it will mean to be without these sacramental items for an extended period of time. Our thanks go to Hermano Carlos, Ysamur and Dorothy Flores-Peña, Felipe and Valeria García-Villamil, Sonia Gastelum, and Charles Guelperin. We also thank the collectors who have graciously lent us objects—Rick and Amber Blanco, Donald Cosentino, Michael Owen Jones, Jim and Jeanne Pieper, Patrick A. Polk, and Jeri Bernadette Williams—and the donors who have given works to our permanent collection—Mrs. Patricia Altman, James H. Kindel Jr., Susan N. Masuoka, Thomas A. McLaughlin, Fred and Barbara Meirs, and Lenore Hoag Mulryan.

This project has been made possible by a number of generous funders, many of whom are long-time friends and patrons of the Fowler. For *Infinito Botánica: L.A.: A Project by Franco Mondini-Ruiz*, we are grateful to Dallas Price-Van Breda and to Shirley and Ralph Shapiro for their help in an exploration of new realms of contemporary artistic expression. For *Botánica Los Angeles: Latino Popular Religious Art in the City of Angels*, we wish to acknowledge support from the Donald B. Cordry Memorial Fund, Jim and Jeanne Pieper, Monica Salinas, the

Yvonne Lenart Public Programs Fund, the UCLA School of the Arts and Architecture, and Manus, the support group of the Fowler Museum.

As is always true, this complex project could not have been realized without the stellar contributions of the entire Fowler Museum staff. They continue to impress me with their professionalism and with their ability to work so effectively as a team. I extend to each and every member my sincere appreciation. Special thanks go to Polly Nooter Roberts, Deputy Director and Chief Curator, who has so ably and graciously handled the coordination and oversight of *Botánica Los Angeles: Latino Popular Religious Art in the City of Angels*. Her curatorial assistant, Gassia Armenian, has been a clear hero of this effort, tackling the myriad details, tracking the numerous items borrowed for the exhibition, and helping to purchase and accumulate many essential botánica commodities. The staffs of the Fowler Registration, Collections, and Conservation Departments—Sarah Kennington, Farida Sunada, Fran Krystock, Jason DeBlock, Jo Hill, and Patricia Measures—have also done their typical excellent job of organizing the flow and movement of objects to, from, and within the Museum, as well as evaluating their exhibition-worthiness. This project has demanded unusual flexibility and patience from them. David Mayo, Director of Exhibitions, is to be commended for creating highly sympathetic installation environments for both exhibition projects. He and his staff bring a wealth of talent and experience to their many complicated tasks. The same is true of the Museum's Education Department, led by Betsy D. Quick—assisted by Ilana Gatti and Trinidad Ruiz—which has developed a rich array of interdisciplinary programs for all the Fowler's audiences. Likewise, fundraising has been creatively pursued by Lynne Brodhead, Director of Development, and her associate Leslie Denk, and publicity and promotion have been strategically conceived by Stacey Ravel Abarbanel, Director of Communications. The administrative staff, under the supervision of David Blair, Assistant Director, has provided crucial support and advice.

This book has been challenging on many fronts, and I congratulate the Publications Department for another remarkable effort under pressing time constraints. Danny Brauer, Director of Publications, has played an active role in identifying and choreographing visual material for the book and has designed it with wit and style. Lynne Kostman, Managing Editor, coordinated this multiauthor volume with her considerable skill and usual diplomacy. The beautiful photography is the work of Don Cole.

Once again, I wish to thank Patrick A. Polk and his many collaborators in this project for opening our eyes to this rich and expressive panoply of religious activity in Los Angeles. It will likely awaken a desire to explore neighborhoods of the city rarely visited and embolden many of us to enter these sanctuaries of spiritual power and artistic imagination. And, finally, the opportunity to present a more ethnographic evocation of botánicas in Los Angeles alongside the visual spectacle of Franco Mondini-Ruiz's artistic interpretation brings a new dimension of dynamism and resonance to our exhibition programming.

Marla C. Berns
Director

ACKNOWLEDGMENTS

Since the day I first walked into a botánica in the mid-1980s, my understanding of the meanings and implications of these shops has been guided by innumerable practitioners, scholars, and acquaintances, more than I could possibly name here. I can only hope that this volume and the accompanying exhibition do justice to the spiritual beliefs, life histories, and hopes of all those who shared with me their perceptions of the botánica and associated religious traditions.

First and foremost, I would like to thank the owners and staff of the many botánicas I have visited and photographed over the years. Their patience and willingness to answer my often uninformed (and sometimes quite silly) questions formed the bedrock of this project. I take full responsibility for any cracks and fissures that may have appeared in the solid foundation they provided.

I am particularly indebted to the artists/practitioners who have taken up the challenge of transforming sections of the UCLA Fowler Museum's Lucas Gallery into evocative reproductions of the sacred spaces found in their botánicas and homes. They and the members of their blood and spiritual families form the heart and soul of the exhibition. So, special thanks—in order of appearance in the book—to Felipe and Valeria García Villamil, their children Ajamu, Tomasa, Miguel, Atoyebi, their granddaughter Divali and spiritual godchildren including Nery Madrid, Oguntoye, and Bob Wisdom; Charley Guelperin, Charles Jablonski, Eve Guelperin, and Nelson López; Sammy and Dorothy Flores-Peña and their son Ariel; Sonia Gastelum, her children Shawn, Sonia, Charlene, and Dee-Dee, her grandchildren Crystal and Hadé, and her assistant Cecilia; Hermano Carlos and family, Oscar Rodriguez and the members of the Cofradía San Simón, and all the celebrants who give life to the annual San Simón celebrations; and last but not least Franco Mondini-Ruiz.

The book and exhibition have benefited greatly from the generosity of a number of individuals who have lent objects for display or who have granted permission to reprint creative works including poetry, paintings, and photographs. *Muchas gracias* to Jim Pieper, Rick and Amber Blanco, Gassia Armenian, Christine Murphey, Michael Owen Jones, Jeri Bernadette Williams, Martin Mayer of Indio Products, Inc., Mike Orta of Saydel, Inc., Sabrina Gledhill, Robert Lentz, Nicholas Jainschigg, Paul Wallfisch, Scott Schaefer, and Sophia Vackimes.

To the authors who contributed to this volume—Donald J. Cosentino, Ysamur Flores-Peña, Miki Garcia, Claudia J. Hernández, Michael Owen Jones, and Yves Marton—I am immensely thankful for your words, your dedication, and your desire to share with others crucial aspects of your research and personal experiences. I am also grateful to many of my colleagues in the former UCLA Folklore and Mythology Program and the new Department of World Arts and Cultures who have enthusiastically supported my research and have shared with me many useful insights. In addition to dialogues with most of the authors mentioned above, especially memorable are conversations with Roberta "Robin" Evanchuk, Bill Perry, Steve Wehmeyer, Kerry Noonan, Tim Correll, and Victoria Simmons.

Grants from the National Center for Complementary and Alternative Medicine, National Institutes of Health (R21-AT00202), as well as from the Harvard Pluralism Project provided much-needed financial aid for the research endeavors of several key collaborators, and on their behalf I would like thank the funding agencies and the translators, transcribers, and research assistants whose efforts where supported by the grants: kudos to West Barbar, Rosa Burciaga, Marisol Castillo, Wennifer Lin Curry, Josué Domínguez, Jules Hart, Rebeca Hernández-Fajardo, Maribel López, Jaynie Rabb, Reyna Ronelli, Rosa Segura, Vanessa Vega, and Alesia Young. Let me also join Marla Berns in acknowledging the hard work, professionalism, and ingenuity of the Fowler Museum's staff. Their supportive enthusiasm and occasional prods were critical at times when my own energy was waning. "Light is the task," so goes the ancient saying, "when many share the toil." How appropriate proverbs such as this are! Indeed, if not for the accumulated wisdom, unique talents, and concerted efforts of many, this project could not have been realized.

Lastly, I owe more to my wife, Jeri, for her love, patience, and assistance than I can repay any time soon, but I promise to keep paying on the principal.

Patrick A. Polk

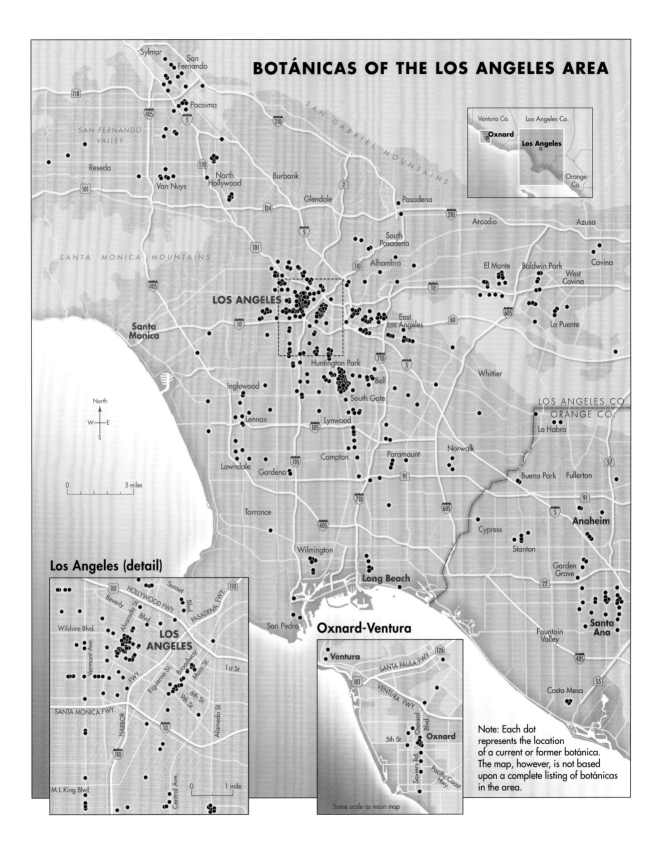

BOTÁNICAS OF THE LOS ANGELES AREA

Ventura Co.   Los Angeles Co.

Oxnard

Los Angeles

Orange Co.

SAN GABRIEL MOUNTAINS

Sylmar
San Fernando
Pacoima
SAN FERNANDO VALLEY
Reseda
Van Nuys
North Hollywood
Burbank
Glendale
Pasadena
Arcadia
Azusa
SANTA MONICA MOUNTAINS
South Pasadena
Alhambra
El Monte
Baldwin Park
Covina
West Covina
LOS ANGELES
East Los Angeles
La Puente
Santa Monica
Whittier
LOS ANGELES CO.
ORANGE CO.
Huntington Park
Inglewood
Bell
South Gate
La Habra
North
W E
S
Lennox
Lynwood
Norwalk
Buena Park
Fullerton
0   5 miles
Lawndale
Gardena
Compton
Paramount
Anaheim
Cypress
Stanton
Garden Grove
Torrance
Fountain Valley
Santa Ana
Wilmington
Long Beach
Costa Mesa
San Pedro

Oxnard-Ventura

Los Angeles (detail)

Sunset
HOLLYWOOD FWY.
PASADENA FWY.
Beverly Blvd.
Alvarado St.
Blvd.
Wilshire Blvd.
Vermont Ave.
LOS ANGELES
FWY.
Broadway
Figueroa St.
Main St.
1st St.
6th St.
9th St.
Alameda St.
SANTA MONICA FWY.
HARBOR
M.L. King Blvd.
Central Ave.
0   1 mile

Ventura
SANTA PAULA FWY.
VENTURA FWY.
5th St.
Saviers Rd.
Oxnard Blvd.
Oxnard
Pacific Coast Hwy.
Same scale as main map

Note: Each dot represents the location of a current or former botánica. The map, however, is not based upon a complete listing of botánicas in the area.

13

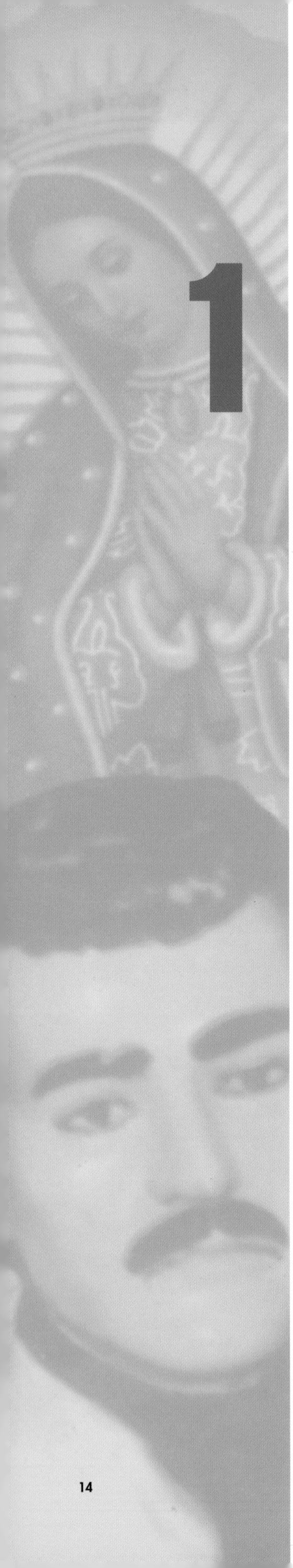

1

BOTÁNICA LOS ANGELES

An Introduction

Patrick Arthur Polk

We bless every door
Every window
With the ether of jasmine
The smoke of basil/albahaca
A candle lit for Eleguá wá wá
Messenger & keeper of all doors
ADRIAN CASTRO (1997)

Voodoo Hoodoo
There Goes the Neighborhood
Voodoo Hoodoo
There Goes the Neighborhood
It got very strange
You saw diff'rent colors
Heard diff'rent sounds
You smelled diff'rent odors
It used to be so nice
It used to be so fine
But since they moved in—
With their voodoo hoodoo
Since they moved in—
DOLORES PRIDA (1991 [1985])

1.1
Botánica storefronts. Photographs
by Patrick A. Polk, Southern
California, 1990–2003.

DOORS AND PERCEPTIONS

The botánica is closed. Peering into the dark interior through the security bars that frame its glass-paneled door and stretch across the undersized front window, I can barely make out the arrangement inside: a counter and several half-stocked shelves, a couple of indistinguishable statues, and sundry other items. It's fairly standard as far as botánicas go; yet the hand-painted sign—"*Botánica Damais y Productos de Belleza*"—has peaked my interest, and so I lean closer to the facade to get a better look. I've done this at other places during off-hours, but it still feels awkward, as if I'm more akin to a Peeping Tom than a window-shopper or ethnographic researcher. Suddenly, as if on cue, I'm startled by an inquisitive voice from behind me. María Galván, the owner, has pulled up and parked her car at the curb. Even before shutting the driver's-side door she calls out, "Can I help you?" The question addresses her concerns more than mine. When I explain that I'm documenting botánicas in Southern California, she hesitates as if expecting some all too familiar and unwelcome line of inquiry. I reassure her that I'm only interested in the shop because I'm developing an exhibition of religious arts associated with botánicas. In other words, I'm not a reporter looking for a juicy story. I'm not a police officer. I'm not a missionary or a health inspector. Nor am I a potential competitor spying on her setup. I'm just an ethnographer. Not that that doesn't come with its own set of problems. My business card and a plastic binder filled with my photographs of shrines at other botánicas help to convince her of my sincerity. She unlocks the door and I follow her inside.

"So what exactly is it you want to know?" she inquires with the disinterested and hurried demeanor of a businesswoman who feels unnecessary chatter is wasting her time. I tell her that my main question is a simple one, "What is a botánica?" Neither of us vocalizes it, but we both know well enough it's a complicated matter. María's response is appropriately vague yet still to the point, "It's a place of mysteries." She then quickly adds, "It depends on what you're looking for." I reiterate that the sacred objects—chromolithographs, statues, and shrines—intrigue me. Without looking up, she crumbles a bit of powdered incense into a censor, lights it with a stick match, and spreads the rising wisps of smoke around the front of the shop. Shrugging her shoulders, she states, "I only work with good spirits, like that Indian over there." Turning around, I note a small statue of a Native American, complete with feathered warbonnet, sitting cross-legged by the entrance. "He protects the store and keeps trouble

1.2
Botánica Damais. Photograph by Patrick A. Polk, Central Los Angeles, 2004.

1.3
This statue representing a Native American guardian spirit is situated near the front door of Botánica Damais. Photograph by Patrick A. Polk, Central Los Angeles, 2004.

1.4
The primary Native American spirit of María Galván, proprietor of Botánica Damais. Photograph by Patrick A. Polk, Central Los Angeles, 2004.

outside," she says in a more lively tone. "He's beautiful," I respond. "May I take a picture of him?" She nods approval. Kneeling down in front of the guardian, I take several photos. A threshold has been crossed. By the time I stand up, María has already brought out a large plaster bust depicting a different Native American, one that she had hidden behind the counter. "This is a special one," she confides. "He's my favorite *indio*."

I snap a few shots as she looks on proudly and then follow her around the botánica. Her primary spiritual guides are located in the shop's back room along with her consultation desk. Stationed on a table covered with a white cloth and surrounded by candles and glasses filled with clear water, are statues of Saint Jude, the patron of the hopeless, San Simón, the Guatemalan trickster saint, and Jesús Malverde, the martyred Robin Hood of the U.S./Mexico borderland. María seems pleased when I name the latter two before she has a chance to tell me who they are. Apologizing for the messy appearance of the space, she lets me photograph the altar where she does her spiritual work (*trabajo espiritual*). The embarrassing clutter consists mostly of plastic or paper bags containing candles encased in glass, vials of scented oil, and other ritual items she employs on behalf of her clients. Not wanting to take too much of her time on this initial meeting, I thank María for her patience and prepare to leave. She wonders aloud if I'm going to make her famous. Only then do I actually inquire as to her name. It's a habit borne out of experience rather than timidity or forgetfulness. She readily offers it but betrays still-lingering doubts by following up with, "This won't get me in trouble, will it?" I assure her that it will not. María then surprises me by commenting that it doesn't matter anyway because she's selling the botánica. No reason is given. She also refuses to reveal what the term *Damais* in the name of the shop

1.5
María Galván's spiritual altar featuring statues of San Judas, San Simón, and Jesús Malverde. Photograph by Patrick A. Polk, Botánica Damais, Central Los Angeles, 2004.

means but makes it clear that it has a special significance. I try pressing the issue. She just flashes a slight smile and shakes her head silently.

María's minimal definition of her botánica as "a place of mysteries" discloses the metaphysical appreciation of *mystery* as a synonym for *spirit* and *divinity*. Botánicas *are* mysterious. And this is not just because they're traditionally allied with the still exotic Afro-Cuban faiths Santería and Palo Mayombé, as well as other Latin American folk traditions including Espiritismo and spirit-inspired healing, or Curanderismo (see chapter 3 of this volume). Mystery is characteristic of spiritual centers in general. Places that cater to the long-held as well as newly received beliefs of untold thousands of people can't avoid evincing a certain mystique, irrespective of the cultural or ethnic backgrounds of the worshipers. Catholic cathedrals, Buddhist temples, and Jewish synagogues surely inspire a similar sense of awe and wonderment on the part of first-time entrants and lifelong devotees. It's a crucial aspect of sacred spaces that starts with the architecture and works its way down to the brass furnishings. Always present is a structural or decorative element—a door, a passageway, a shaded nook, a gilded box, or a piece of drapery that rustles when people walk by—that seems to conceal a sacrament whose form and essence can only be revealed to those who are ready.

María's pronouncement on the nature of her shop is equally in tune with the common understanding of *mystery* as a puzzle, problem, or dilemma. For this very reason, botánicas have been aptly termed "curative promises" (Fernández Olmos and Paravisini-Gebert 2001). Images of the Blessed Virgin, martyred saints, African gods, Native American warriors, and corpulent Buddhas all have knowable purposes or potencies. When sacralized through ritual action, these tangible visions of otherworldly forces offer the possibility of spiritually rewarding, emotionally empowering, and physically healing experiences. Speaking of the contents of botánicas and the necessity of informed human agency to vitalize the objects, Joseph Murphy writes, "To the uninitiated, their merchandise must look mysterious indeed: candles and beads, herbs and oils, cauldrons and crockery, and plaster statues of Catholic saints. Yet for those who know their meaning, each of these items has a part to play in santería" (1988, 39). Echoing this perspective, art historian David Brown remarks, "All together, in a single retail space, these eye-popping curiosities might resist identification and narratives of unity to the untrained eye, unless one were ethnocentric enough to consign them to the waste bin of urban kitsch" (2003, 1). In the eyes of believers and seekers, the botánica is a place where gods, saints, and guiding spirits may be encountered first in frozen material form and then harnessed via more actively corporeal modes of symbolic communication.

Botánicas are also mysterious in the sense that they are often perceived by outsiders as the most effective entry point into barely comprehensible and out-of-the-ordinary magical realms that have been transplanted from faraway places. This essay itself relies on a literary strategy commonly employed by ethnographers, journalists, and narrators of mystical autobiographies—namely the portrayal of an initial entry into a botánica as the starting point of a journey toward cultural understanding, spiritual enlightenment, or self-discovery. Time and time again, readers are walked though botánica entranceways and forced to share in an author's experience of delight, discomfort, or disorientation. Anthropologist Raquel Romberg describes her first foray into a Puerto Rican botánica: "Hesitantly, as a strange sense of the unknown—both tempting and frightening—takes hold of me, I enter a botánica for the first time. Browsing over shelves and pretending to be at ease, I try to understand what I am experiencing—but to no avail" (2003, 81). Ultimately, for Romberg, the oddness and unorthodoxy of the shop are made sensible through the close and complex personal relationships she develops with proprietors and the self-proclaimed witch-healers (*brujos*) who make use of the products.

1.6
Science fiction and fantasy illustrator Nicholas Jainschigg has been fascinated with the magic and mystery of botánicas since his childhood in Manhattan. He used to go to a nearby shop and pepper the owner with questions about artifacts and items for sale, including a jar full of dried tarantulas. Here he imagines what might happen if other, more fantastic, creatures preserved in jars came to life and escaped (personal communication, 2004). From *Weird Tales Magazine* (spring 1993), no. 206. Reproduced with permission of the artist. Photograph by Don Cole.

Less-receptive observers, particularly those whose imaginations are fed on popular American racial fantasies, may envision scenes of black magic and frightful "native" rites beyond the doors of the botánica. Reinforced by rumors insinuating links to Satanism, drug trafficking, and even catastrophic forest fires, members of the clergy, eager news reporters, and "concerned citizens" condemn the insidious behaviors supposedly engaged in by botánica owners or their clienteles. Operatives for People for the Ethical Treatment of Animals (PETA) have been advised to stake out the shops in order to identify animal abusers, probably jockeying for vantage points with cult-awareness specialists who make their livings lecturing to police departments and neighborhood watch associations. One officer describes efforts to investigate a botánica, "Every time we would go out there, we thought they had a look-see man. It was like going to a gambling house. There's always that one. That's how this place was" (Kahaner 1988, 115). Perspectives such as these explain why some botánica operators duck for cover when people with notebooks and tape recorders head their way, while others step up and try to "set the record straight."

In many ways, botánicas are *not at all* mysterious. They have regular hours of operation. They have business licenses. Their advertisements in newspapers or on printed handbills offer family discounts and two-for-one specials. They sell books, candles, bath oils, incense, prayer cards, saint's statues, rosaries, shampoos, jewelry, clothing, and a wide variety of other mundane articles—most of which

1.7
Rick Blanco. *La Botánica de Juana*, 1997. Acrylic on canvas. 61 x 91 cm. As this painting by Cuban American artist Rick Blanco illlustrates, a botánica was and frequently still is a place where people buy herbs and other medicinal remedies. Collection of Amber and Rick Blanco. Reproduced with permission of the artist. Photograph by Artworks, Pasadena, California.

are purchased from wholesalers who furnish these same items to Catholic gift shops, Christian bookstores, and other less symbolically laden retail businesses. The botánicas registered in telephone and business directories—and most are listed—may be found under a wide range of well-known headings: beauty salons, candle shops, florists, herbalists, gift shops, occult stores, suppliers of religious articles, variety stores, and so on. Because the proprietors offer advice and therapy—spiritual or otherwise—they may also fall under the rubrics of "Alternative Healthcare Practitioners," "Self-Help Counselors," "Psychics," and "Spiritual Advisors." In other words, much of what happens in a botánica is exceedingly commonplace—especially in California—even if it does resist easy categorization.

Botánicas are also familiar in that for many clients they support the continuation of homeland traditions within the context of Diaspora, immigration, and exile. As such, they are markers of identity signifying cultural presence and continuity. Where you find botánicas, you find Cubanos, Nuyoricans, Dominicanos, Tainos, Aztecas, Mexicanos, and Guatemaltecos or at least evidence of their increasing impact on the cultural landscape of contemporary America. To some extent, botánicas do offer "a refuge from a much colder world outside" (Murphy 1988, 48) by providing a recognizable and acceptable zone in which customary belief can be freely expressed. They may also inspire nostalgia and fond memories of a time when the visual and ritual aspects of faith weren't confined to narrow market spaces in the low-rent urban shopping centers of North America.

Even more, botánicas may become idealized as sites of resurgent cultural vitality and resistance. Some Mexican American intellectuals and activists claim the shops as part of Aztlán, the metaphoric Chicano homeland that extends deep into the heart of North America. To be sure, the very same pesticide-laced Oxnard streets in which César Chávez first struggled to unite farmworkers now boast nearly a dozen botánicas. Work in the fields is still a backbreaking occupation, one where poverty-level wages and insufficient or nonexistent medical coverage are typical. As a result botánicas are increasingly relied upon as economically and culturally accessible health care alternatives. It is proudly noted that on Whittier Boulevard in East L.A. descendants of Moctezuma can still buy herbal remedies that were in use long before steel-encased conquistadors stumbled off their disease-ridden caravels with starving horses in tow (Chabrán 1997, 3). A Puerto Rican American actress and dancer who goes by the nickname "La Bruja" claims, "The Botanica holds possibly our last connection to our spiritual foundations, where nature was valued before gold" (De La Luz, 2004). What else are all those Native American statues stationed near botánica entryways trying to keep out? Or keep in?

Conversely, botánicas may represent places of assimilation, where practitioners actively try to bring the folk traditions of their homelands into better alignment with broader American expectations. Many shop owners seek to maintain some traditional practices while at the same time experimenting with new ways of visualizing the sacred and addressing the needs of customers. Reacting to the bewilderment and trepidation expressed by potential clients, some have outfitted their botánicas to appear more like mainstream medical clinics or counselors' offices. "You can't help them," remarks one, "if you can't get them in the door." In addition to tarot card readings and spiritual cleansings, another presents lectures with titles like "The Power of Positive Thinking" and "Public Speaking Made Easy." The repackaging and reshaping of behavior in response to cultural and marketplace pressures is not without detractors. The owner of one long-established shop proclaims, "A botánica is just supposed to be a place to sell religious articles. That's it. Not all this other stuff."

The distinction between fitting in and selling out is a fine one, as is that between cooperating and co-opting. Trendy boutiques in Venice Beach and Silver Lake and on Melrose Avenue have created mini-botánicas, playing on the pop culture and kitsch value of the products if nothing else. Predicting one possible outcome of this increasingly complex cultural interplay, an irreverent commentator divines:

> As mid-America and its suburbs become increasingly multicultural, Hispanic followers of Santeria and Voudoun are no longer found only in the inner cities or places like New Orleans. Botanicas, those do-it-yourself supply shops where followers of the saints can purchase Orisha effigies, candles, herbs, John the Conqueror roots, and jinx removing powders, begin to appear in suburban shopping malls alongside the Hallmark card galleries. Before long the Anglophone middle class takes up this folk religion and an enterprising team of MBAS founds a successful chain of unthreatening and antiseptic botanicas called Mojo-Meister, Inc. [Kinney 1999–2001]

The movement falls to ruin, however, when "the Mojo-Meister chain's officers are indicted in an insider stock selloff scandal" (Kinney 1999–2001). The scenario

1.8
Display shelf at Botánica Nueva Esperanza with Buddha, Jesús Malverde, Scooby-Doo, Cookie Monster, and other imported ceramic icons. Photograph by Patrick A. Polk, Huntington Park, 2004.

is tongue-in-cheek, but the potential dilemma is real. What will it mean when botánicas are no longer Cuban, Puerto Rican, Dominican, Taino, Aztec, Mexican, or Guatemalan, but rather just American? It depends on what "American" comes to mean in the future.

Within the botánicas and the alternative metaphysical perspectives most closely associated with them, mainstream and subaltern identities, histories, and mythologies are routinely conflated and deconstructed in ironic, and sometimes comedic, ways. Referring to a botánica in Havana, the Cuban novelist Alejo Carpentier once wrote, "Here you find surrealism in its brute force" (1981, 336), implying that colonialism's apparent losers are artistically reshaping and spiritually resisting the miswritten histories of its victors.

So who are the people that operate botánicas? Expatriates and immigrants who found that national boundaries and transnational migrations didn't change a person's need to connect with the divine and realized that someone had to provide the material components of faith: They are gray-haired Cubans who fled the island in the late 1950s; younger and generally darker-skinned Cubans who got out in the Mariel boatlifts of the early 1980s; Puerto Ricans who left their island too; Mexicans and Central Americans who know there isn't a nearby town square where you can find a wizened *india* selling sacramental objects from a booth cobbled together with old wooden planks; Mexican Americans whose *tías* used to be that old woman; a Colombian with a light complexion and European features claiming to be an Amazonian Indian and whose botánica franchise has at least twelve locations in carefully selected neighborhoods around Southern California; a woman from El Salvador who was raised in L.A. and found faith when she needed it most; a Peruvian couple who tend the houseplants they sell just as lovingly as they do their statues of Catholic saints; gay men and women who know that the behavioral rules of the spirit world trump those of the everyday;

1.9
Cover art from the debut album of Botanica, an alternative rock band fronted by Paul Wallfisch. Reproduced with permission of Paul Wallfisch, Botanica, and Scott Schaefer, Checkered Past Records. Photograph by Gregg Segal, 1999.

and people who look to what they know best as a means of securing a foothold in an economy built on cultural consumption—it's either a botánica or a restaurant.

Who patronizes botánicas? Most customers are Latinos, but the full clientele of each shop tends to reflect the broad cultural and ethnic diversity of its neighborhood. Included are immigrants who carried miniature statues of El Santo Niño with them when they crossed the Florida Strait or the Rio Grande and owe him a lighted candle for his vigilance; *braceros*, or day laborers, from Guatemala seeking remedies for problems they thought they left behind and dilemmas they didn't expect to find here; perfectly coiffed Cuban matrons who lost their husbands either to the Revolution or the long angry wait for it to fail and now argue the fine points of a religion they didn't practice when La Habana was free; a haggard-looking African American prostitute in a short skirt who hides just inside the door of a botánica because someone has threatened her and then watches the proprietor fuss over the multilayered dress worn by a doll dedicated to the spirit of a Black female slave; Jewish fathers who come to ask for help with family problems they wouldn't dare share with their rabbis; Filipinos who can't find their brand of Catholicism being practiced here and stop by for items the church doesn't sell; and young transvestites who wander in off Santa Monica Boulevard and find solace in the botánica of a *santero* who assures them that "God didn't make a mistake. There is love and a place for you in this world." Elsewhere, another shopkeeper decries how the homosexuals are ruining the religion and then tallies the number of candles he sells to crimson-haired Goths wearing black nail polish. Still other owners regale you with tales of which Hollywood movie stars and Grammy award-winning musicians walked into whose botánica first. Finally, there's the nondescript person who quietly enters the botánica, buys a special item, and hurries away.

As with their owners and clienteles, botánicas resist generalized characterizations. Much like the city of Los Angeles itself, they are rendered almost indefinable by the largely unprecedented intercultural environment in which they exist. Where do official and unofficial boundaries really start and stop? Where is the conceptual center? Nearly irreconcilable street-level perceptions of what a botánica is can be revealed by traversing just a few short blocks from one shop to another. Ultimately, the one certain thing about botánicas is that they are becoming an increasingly visible component of city life. Among other things, botánicas are a public face of Santería, Palo Mayombé, Espiritismo, and Curanderismo. They are also rapidly becoming the most accessible purveyors of items used by practitioners of Wicca and other Neo-Pagan traditions, African American conjure and rootwork, New Orleans-style Voodoo, New Agers, naturopaths, homeopaths, occultists of all stripes, and good Catholics from all parts of the globe. Popular women's health books, community medical programs sponsored by major universities, and studies supported by the National Institutes of Health all promote botánicas as culturally appropriate healthcare providers, variously referring to them as "invisible hospitals" and "poor-man's pharmacies."

Botánicas give evidence of the divine manifested in everyday life; they enable practitioners to develop personal relationships with sacred powers; they assist individuals in dealing with their immediate existential needs; and they encapsulate key notions of cultural, ethnic, and regional or national identity. Additionally they help to maintain cultural values and familial relationships across generations; serve as resources for explaining suffering and death; function as a basis for crafting responses to oppression and social equality; and present a means of making sense out of cultural displacement and transnational migration by filtering the experience of border crossing through the prism of mythology and hagiography. They offer ritual and herbal therapies for a variety of physical and mental health conditions. They can be a good place to sit and gossip, catch up with old acquaintances, or just to cool off on a warm day. And beyond all this, what is a botánica? Well, it all depends on what you're looking for.

VISIONS OF THE SACRED: AN OVERVIEW OF THE VOLUME

The orientation that primarily informs this volume is the understanding of botánicas as symbolically and ritually charged sites where identities and faiths are transmitted, transformed, and critiqued largely through the importation, adaptation, and recycling of religious imagery. Taking as our chief subject the altars, shrines, icons, and other ritual paraphernalia assembled and displayed in botánicas or at the homes of practitioners, we seek to illuminate the ongoing processes of cultural synthesis that are reworking the religious and social landscapes of urban America and, in particular, Los Angeles. In this way, we exemplify essential aspects of the constantly evolving and intricately intertwined sacred universes into which botánicas are very much gateways. Each of the studies presented here explores how individuals draw on communal traditions, personal memories, and unique aesthetic sensibilities to forge meaningful and rewarding experiences—mystical, therapeutic, cathartic, artistic, socially empowering—for themselves and others.

In the essay entitled "Objects of Devotion," I outline the main religious and healing traditions encountered in botánicas and describe the spiritual essences—gods, saints, and supernatural guides—that serve as foci for visual artistry and ritual behavior. In the following essay, Claudia J. Hernández and Michael Owen Jones offer an introduction to the modes of therapeutic and curative practice most commonly employed by healers working out of botánicas. Subsequent chapters provide detailed explorations of the ways individuals conceptualize and express their religiosity through a wide range of traditional behaviors, including narrative, ritual, and the material representation of specific spiritual entities. First, I describe a throne (*trono*) for Eleguá, a chief divinity (*oricha*) within Santería. Created by Afro-Cuban priest and master drummer Felipe García

Villamil and his wife, Valeria, this ornate shrine embodies crucial notions of spiritual power and the visual presence of the divine. Then, in his heartfelt tribute to the late América Leyva, a pioneer botánica owner in Los Angeles, Yves Marton gives a deeply personal account of how his dialogue with and subsequent mentorship by América impacted not only his academic work but also his own spirituality and his emotional and physical well-being. Next, drawing on his study of Charles (Charley) Guelperin, an *espiritista* who operates Botánica El Congo Manuel, Donald J. Cosentino explores the underpinnings of the metaphysical link between spiritualists and the spirits they channel. Can one separate the guided from the guide?

Embracing Espiritismo as a cultural and family tradition, Ysamur (Sammy) Flores-Peña describes its spiritual principles and material focal points as he and his wife, Dorothy, practice it. Continuing with the theme of how individuals negotiate personal experience, relationships with blood relatives, and the needs of clients, I discuss the spiritual practices of botánica owner Sonia Gastelum and illustrate how her close affinity for three female divinities—Michaela, Irak, and Ochún—reveals key conceptualizations and narratives of self. The article by Polk and Jones on Hermano Carlos and San Simón looks at similar issues in the context of Guatemalan folk Catholicism and then expands the discussion by considering the broader implications of a community festival that takes place annually at Hermano Carlos's botánica.

Lastly, in an essay entitled "Infinite Gestures: Franco Mondini-Ruiz's *Infinito Botánica: L.A.*," Miki Garcia reviews the work of artist Franco Mondini-Ruiz who brings a unique aesthetic sensibility—honed in law school and the Tejano knickknack stores of San Antonio—to Southern California. Inspired by the transnational implications of botánicas, Mondini-Ruiz uses their captivating baroque iconography as a means of addressing how faith, ethnicity, and personal experience are expressed in the rapidly expanding borderlands of America. ❦

2

OBJECTS OF DEVOTION

Sacramental Imagination and the Sacred Universe of the Botánica

Patrick Arthur Polk

We all have a good spirit that is with us from the moment we are born. And he is our protector.

ALLAN KARDEC (1996)

Spend a few hours driving around the City of Angels, and you will quickly realize that material expressions of spiritual belief are an integral component of the urban landscape. Cathedrals, temples, churches, and shrines, immense and tiny, dot the metropolitan grid, placing religious imagery at the most important nodes of residential and commercial activity. But there are many other sites, perhaps even more important ones, where notions of the divine, or at least the supernatural, are made visible. Peer more closely at the facades of businesses, schools, community centers, and other public areas. Glance at the ornamented bumpers, rearview mirrors, and dashboards of the vehicles of fellow commuters. Stop at one of the many local street festivals, demonstrations, or community gatherings that occur on almost any given day. Walk around an unfamiliar neighborhood. Stroll around your own block. Visit a friend or relative and gaze more closely at their living room, dining room, or kitchen. Contemplate your mantelpiece, bedroom, or most private space. The signifying and situating of the sacred through material behavior, a process variously described as "sacramentality" (Hufford 1985), "sacred materiality" (Primiano 1999), "visual piety" (Morgan 1998), or more broadly as "sacramental imagination" (Miller 2004), seem to be a nearly essential social and personal activity. Accordingly, our communal and home environments are replete with religious art, icons, holy

2.1
Botánica y Templo San Simón de los Llanos. Photograph by Patrick A. Polk, Los Angeles, 2000.

26

2.2
Botanica Santa Philomena,
Port-au-Prince, Haiti. A Haitian
who had lived in New York
and had become familiar with
botánicas there established this
shop. Photograph by Patrick A.
Polk, 1995.

2.3
Interior of Botanica Santa
Philomena. Photograph by
Patrick A. Polk, Port-au-Prince,
Haiti, 1995.

images, and other visual components of faith, some strictly orthodox and others fantastically idiosyncratic.

The ability to see God or spirit in or through artifacts and everyday objects routinely manifests itself in the most familiar as well as the most unexpected places: crowded freeways, suburban housing tracts, downtown shopping districts, cramped office cubicles, sites of tragic accidents or brutal crimes, and so on. But where do all the guardian angels, broken-tusked Ganeshas, beatific saints, smiling Buddhas, concerned Madonnas, Gaeas, Kwan Yins, mezuzahs, crucifixes, crescent moons, Stars of David, peaceful doves, happy cats, Jesus fishes, penta-grams, Conquering Lions of Judah, mystic pyramids, golden pagodas, and the whole host of other spiritually evocative images widely displayed throughout the region come from? To be sure, some are unique, hand-fashioned expressions of piety crafted by individual believers for their own use. Most, however, whether encountered as large ornamental outdoor statues or miniature plastic figurines, seasonal holiday decorations or year-round devotional items, greeting cards or window decals, expensive pieces of jewelry or cheap plastic key chain decora-tions, are commercial products supplied by innumerable merchants including denominational religious stores, occult shops, neighborhood ethnic markets, large grocery chains, chic art galleries, tony import-export dealers, kitschy curio shops, desperate street vendors, and sundry other retailers or wholesalers.

2.4
Throughout Latin America, small stores such as this are familiar suppliers of Catholic icons, pilgrimage souvenirs, and other religious articles. In Brazil they are closely associated with African-inspired religions, such as Umbanda and Candomblé. Photograph by Sabrina Gledhill, Salvador da Bahia, Brazil, 2004.

2.5
Interior view of Saravá, a shop specializing in religious articles. Photograph by Sabrina Gledhill, Salvador da Bahia, Brazil, 2004.

Reflecting the broad ethnic and cultural reconfiguration of Southern California in recent years, botánicas are rapidly becoming one of the most familiar purveyors of sacramental items, and their role in supporting and shaping the ways numerous residents, Latino or otherwise, envision and interact with the sacred in everyday life is increasingly obvious. The intent of this chapter is to provide a brief introduction to the religious and therapeutic systems most closely associated with botánicas. It will acquaint the reader with their fundamental metaphysical principles or spiritual essences and the ways in which these inform the use of sacramental items in general and the creation of altars, shrines, and other sacralized environments in particular.

A comprehensive history of the botánica as a mercantile outlet and as a locus of spiritual practice has yet to be written, and the issue can only be addressed here in a general, if not anecdotal, fashion. Most informants intuitively state that the name *botánica* reflects the fact that such shops were, at least initially, "green pharmacies" operated by herbalists in Cuba, or perhaps Puerto Rico, and were later established in North America by expatriates. Others argue that the botánica evolved in the United States—citing New York's Spanish Harlem as its birthplace—and that from there shops spread out across America and even to the Caribbean and Latin America (figs. 2.2, 2.3). Whether they are viewed as a cultural import or an adaptive response on the part of immigrants to a new social environment, it is clear that the majority of the items offered for sale and services

2.6
Images of San Simón and
other sacred figures offered
for sale in San Andrés Itzapa,
Chimaltenango, Guatemala.
Photograph by Jim Pieper, 1991.

rendered at botánicas are strongly reminiscent of, if not directly linked to, folk or homeland traditions of many recently naturalized American citizens, legal residents, and guest or undocumented workers (figs. 2.4–2.6). Additionally, they are analogous to, and in some cases supplant, long-standing North American specialty businesses such as Catholic religious supply houses, occult or metaphysical bookstores, Gypsy palm readers, conjure or hoodoo shops, and herb vendors.

ST. LOUIS CATHEDRAL'S RELIGIOUS STORE
JACKSON SQUARE, NEW ORLEANS
Christine Murphey

A few Mary cards in hand
I search the rack of magnets
for where she stands on the world
sunlight streaming from her palms.

Bernadette rings up a sale—
gives me a nod,
confides it was the cathedral priest
who said marriage vows for Marie Laveau.
My eyebrows raise, appreciate the news
to which she adds
Laveau was not evil.

Priestess-saint religion-crosser,
another Queen to please us all—
her icons in stock:
our whispers below the shelves.

Young girls lean over the counter
comb a pile of medals for St. Jude—
ask who to wear for jobs.
They want to buy St. Cecilia,
know she's worth more than even music.
I'm lucky, find the Black Madonna
and take ten of the Virgin standing barefoot
on the horn of a crescent moon.

With regard to the establishment of botánicas in Southern California, Cubans, Cuban Americans and Puerto Ricans opened the first shops in the late 1950s and early 1960s. Pioneers include: Cubans Nina Pérez, who opened Botánica Nina Religion, and Santos Gil Orta (Professor Márquez), who ran Botánica Santa Bárbara in downtown Los Angeles and later took over Botánica Nina Religion, and the Puerto Rican Ray Pizarro, who founded the Seven Powers Garden Temple Store in South Los Angeles. Over the following decades, however, people from a wide variety of cultural and ethnic backgrounds—generally in successive phases— have found botánicas to be economically and culturally advantageous institutions. The earliest Mexican and Mexican American botánicas seem to date to the late 1960s and early 1970s. In some cases, proprietors of preexisting herb shops, simply exchanged the name *Yerbería* for that of *Botánica*. Guatemalan, Salvadoran, and other Central American storeowners became commonplace in the 1980s and 1990s in keeping with immigration patterns. Here and there, a few African Americans, Asian Americans, and Euro-Americans have established shops as well. At present, it appears that the majority of botánica owners in Southern California are of Mexican or Central American descent, demonstrating the botánica's emergence as a pan-Latino phenomenon.

Although botánica operators may describe themselves using a wide range of titles including professors, experts in folk massage and/or bone-setting techniques (*sobadores*), herbalists (*yerberos*), astrologers (*astrólogos*), parapsychologists (*parasicólogos*), psychics (*psíquicos*), spiritual advisors (*consejeros espirituales*), mentalists (*mentalistas*), occultists (*ocultistas*), and naturopaths (*naturalistas*), the majority of the products offered for sale and the services provided at botánicas are most closely associated with Afro-Cuban religions (Santería and Palo Mayombé); Latin American Spiritist doctrine (Espiritismo); localized, vernacular expressions of Catholic piety (folk Catholicism); and Latin American folk healing or traditional medicine (Curanderismo). Often, the proprietor is a practitioner of several, if not most, of these modalities. For example, folk healers at botánicas almost invariably identify themselves as Catholic. In a similar, hierarchical fashion, it is frequently asserted that one must first be a Catholic and a Spiritist before being initiated as a Santería priest or priestess. For those who are practitioners of both Palo and Santería, a traditional, but not always enforced, stipulation holds that the necessary order of consecration is Palo first and never the other way around.

SANTERÍA

Ultimately derived from the spiritual traditions of the Yoruba of southwestern Nigeria and Benin, Santería is also known variously as *oricha* (*orisha*) worship, Lucumí (an ethnonym used in Cuba to identify peoples of Yoruba ancestry), or Regla de Ocha (Way of the *orichas*). Adherents recognize a pantheon of divinities known as *orichas* or saints (*santos*) who preside over fundamental aspects of the natural environment and human experience (fig. 2.7). Because mortals cannot have direct contact with the Supreme Being (Olodumaré), they must rely on and interact with the *orichas*. Initiation into the priesthood, often a lengthy and expensive undertaking, is seen as an important step toward the fulfillment of

2.7
Popular chromolithograph of
"The Seven African Powers"
depicting the Catholic avatars
of key Santería *orichas*.

2.8
Shrine for the ancestors (*egun*)
at the home of Felipe García
Villamil fashioned according
to Santería or Lucumí tradition.
Photograph by Patrick A. Polk,
Central Los Angeles, 2003.

one's destiny and the deriving of benefit from the spiritual energy (*aché*) of
the universe. Upon initiation, often referred to as being "crowned" or "making
one's saint," priests (*santeros*) or priestesses (*santeras*) assume responsibility
for establishing and maintaining proper ritual relationships with the *orichas* on
their own behalves, for family members, and for those who seek their advice and
services as practitioners. This is primarily accomplished through the observation
of ritual prescriptions and prohibitions, making sacrificial offerings (*ebós*), divination, calendrical celebrations at which time the *orichas* may manifest via spirit
mediumship, fetes in honor of one's ancestors (*egun*), and other rites that demonstrate piety and recognize the continuing presence of the divine in the lives of
worshipers (fig. 2.8).

　　Although most practitioners of Santería maintain that the *orichas* are numerous, if not innumerable, in practice only a dozen or so divinities are regularly
listed as the most important or chief members of the pantheon (see box, pp. 33,
34). Each is honored and invoked with his or her own unique chants, songs, and
drum patterns, and each is associated with sacred days and numbers; favorite foods
and sacrificial offerings; and special colors and symbols. Material representations
drawn primarily from African and European (primarily Catholic) sources give a
visual presence to the *orichas* especially during ceremonies.

THE MAIN *ORICHAS*

Listed below are the *orichas* most often invoked by practitioners along with basic descriptions of their characteristics, sacred symbols, and icons.

BABALÚ AYÉ

God of illness, especially viral diseases and skin conditions, and patron of outcasts, Babalú Ayé's symbol is a broom-like implement that can sweep away pestilence. His colors include yellow, purple, and brown, and his Catholic counterpart is Saint Lazarus.

CHANGÓ

Lord of thunder, lightning, and fire, Changó is a fiercely masculine figure whose primary symbol is the double-headed axe. His colors are red and white, and he is often represented as Saint Barbara.

ELEGUÁ (ELEGBA)

Trickster, messenger of the *orichas*, guardian of all paths, crossroads, and thresholds, Eleguá straddles the seemingly contradictory forces of creation and destruction. His colors are red and black, and his main implement is a hooked staff (*garabato*). He is often represented by a conical cement head with cowries for its eyes and mouth. He may also be depicted as the Holy Child of Atocha or Saint Anthony of Padua.

OBATALÁ

The first *oricha* created by Olodumaré, Obatalá fashioned the world as we know it. A wise and compassionate patriarch and a calming influence for adherents, his color is white, and his symbols include the snail and a white horsetail switch. He is often associated with Our Lady of Mercy and the Immaculate Conception.

2.9
Babalú Ayé/San Lázaro at Botánica El Congo Manuel. Photograph by Don Cole, Hollywood, 2004.

2.10
Eleguá/El Santo Niño de Atocha at Botánica El Congo Manuel. Photograph by Patrick A. Polk, Hollywood, 2003.

2.11
Changó. Detail of throne (*trono*) with icons of the thunder divinity in the home of Felipe García Villamil. Photograph by Patrick A. Polk, Central Los Angeles, 2003.

OCHOSI

Master hunter, scout, sentinel, and guardian, this warrior spirit's key symbols include bows and arrows, deer horns, shields, badges, and handcuffs—all of which are usually placed in a special terra-cotta container. His primary color is blue, and he is often portrayed as the Archangel Michael or Saint Norbert.

OGÚN

Inventor of the forge and worker of iron, Ogún is the ideal soldier, personifying strength, single-minded determination, and the ability to sweep away all obstacles from the path. His implements, primarily fashioned from metal, include machetes, knives, keys, and railroad spikes, all of which are placed in a special three-legged cauldron. His Catholic incarnations include Saint Peter and Saint James the Elder (Santiago).

OCHÚN

Goddess of love, desire, and sensuality, Ochún is the principle of rivers, lakes, and fresh or "sweet" waters. Her main color is gold, and her symbols include mirrors, hand fans, peacock feathers, and copper bracelets. Her Catholic avatar is Our Lady of Charity of Cobre (Caridad del Cobre).

OYÁ

Essence of storms, winds, and tempests, Oyá is an archetypical female warrior and the guardian of the cemetery. Her sacred colors, often nine in number, include maroon, orange, green, yellow, and the hues of the rainbow. She is often associated with Saint Theresa.

OSAIN

Divine herbalist and giver of medicinal plants, Osain's symbols include a gourd decorated with beads of various colors and an anthropomorphic figure with one eye, one arm, and one hand. Sometimes he is depicted as Saint John, Saint Joseph, or Saint Ambrose.

LOS IBEYI

Twin child *orichas* known as Taiwo and Kainde are the protectors of children and bringers of youthful joy, good fortune, and prosperity. They are often represented with twin dolls or images of the saints Cosmas and Damian.

ORUNMILA (ALSO ORÚNLA OR ORULA)

Archetypal diviner, Orunmila is the master of the Ifá divination tray and patron of *babalawos*, priests specially trained in the techniques of Ifá divination. His colors are green and yellow, and his Catholic counterpart is usually Saint Francis of Assisi.

YEMAYÁ

Ideal mother figure, giver of life, and mistress of the seas, Yemayá's colors are blue, crystal, and coral; and her metal, silver. She is often depicted as the Virgin of Regla or as a mermaid.

2.12
Product labels featuring key emblems of selected *orichas*. Reproduced with permission of Indio Products, Inc.

REGLAS DE KONGO OR REGLAS DE PALO

The terms Reglas de Kongo (Ways of the Kongo) or Reglas de Palo (Ways of Palo) are used to refer to several branches of Central African-derived religion that evolved in Cuba, most notably Palo Mayombé or Palo Monte, Palo Kimbisa, and Palo Briyumba. Each system has somewhat different theological and ritual orientations, but their close cultural and historical relations to one another enable them to be widely viewed as "branches of the same tree." Practitioners of Palo (*paleros/as* or *mayomberos/as*) postulate the existence of a creator deity, Nzambi, who like Olodumaré of Santería, is a distant and largely unapproachable divinity. Thus, adherents place emphasis on working with a range of spiritual essences including environmental elements (trees, plants, rocks, animals), deified forces of nature (such as wind, earthquakes, and lightning), and divine ancestors— all variously referred to as *nkisi* or *mpungos*. Among the most commonly recognized *nkisi* are Lucero (divine messenger and master of the crossroads), Sarabanda (principle of iron, warfare, employment, and self-protection; fig. 2.13), Tiembla Tierra (creator of the world, force of peace and harmony), Siete Rayos (thunder, lighting, fire), and Madre Agua (life-giving waters and maternity). Practitioners

2.13
Palo *nganga* (an iron pot filled with and surrounded by sacred objects) for the *nkisi* (spirit) Sarabanda at the home of Felipe García Villamil. Photograph by Patrick A. Polk, Central Los Angeles, 2003.

often suggest direct correlations between characteristics and functions of primary *nkisi* and the *orichas* of Santería. Additionally, and, perhaps most importantly, *paleros* work with the spirits of the dead, known as *muertos* or *nfumbes*, who serve as mentors, spiritual guides, and guardian angels, among other things.

Following a series of incremental initiations, *paleros* earn the right to own and construct an *nganga* or *prenda*, an iron pot filled with dry branches (*palos*), vines, roots, animal bones, tools, and other objects that symbolize nature and the spiritual attributes of the *muertos* and *nkisi* with whom they work. Through the maintenance of the shrines, they are able to call upon these entities for assistance in a variety of spiritual matters. Historically, Palo has been a much more secretive practice than Santería, if only because the emphasis on the dead often leads outsiders to label it derogatorily as witchcraft or black magic. Accordingly, Palo *ngangas* and *prendas* are often hidden away in botánicas or kept at home, and, as a result, Kongo-derived practices are generally the least evident aspects of the visual display of the sacred within shops.

2.14 (top left)
Doll representing a spirit guide who was a nun during her earthly life. Photograph by Patrick A. Polk, Botánica Orula, Lynwood, 2004.

2.15 (top right)
The spiritual altar, or *bóveda*, of Felipe García Villamil. Photograph by Patrick A. Polk, Central Los Angeles, 2004.

2.16 (bottom left)
Espiritismo shrine for archetypal male and female African spirits at Botánica Nina Religion, Los Angeles. Photograph by Patrick A. Polk, circa 1992.

2.17 (bottom right)
Interior of Botánica Eleggua, Lynwood, with statue of an African or Congo spirit. Photograph by Patrick A. Polk, 2003.

2.18
Indian guides at Botánica
Divino Niño Jesús, Huntington
Park. Photograph by Patrick A.
Polk, 2004.

2.19
Gypsy spirit (doll) at Botánica
El Congo Manuel, Hollywood.
Photograph by Don Cole, 2004.

2.20
A statue of the Buddha in
Botánica Nueva Esperanza,
Huntington Park. Photograph by
Patrick A. Polk, 2004.

ESPIRITISMO

Many, if not most, botánica owners identify themselves as Spiritists (*espiritistas*) referencing a specific spiritual doctrine, while others will broadly term themselves spiritual advisors (*consejos espirituales*) or simply state that they do spiritual work (*trabajo espiritual*). *Espiritistas* follow the European Spiritist tradition established by Allan Kardec (the pseudonym of Léon-Denizard-Hippolyte Rivail [1804–1869]). Kardec authored a series of metaphysical tracts outlining a doctrine of Spiritism, the most influential of which—*The Spirits' Book*, *The Mediums' Book*, and *The Collection of Prayers*—have enjoyed great popularity throughout Latin America, especially in Cuba, Puerto Rico, and Brazil. Kardec expressed the view that "Spirit interactions with human beings can be either subtle or direct. The subtle communications happen without our awareness, generally in the form of inspiration. We need to exercise discernment, however, in distinguishing between the uplifting and the malevolent kinds. Direct exchanges occur through writing, speech, and other physical manifestations, usually with the intervention of a medium who acts as a link between the two worlds" (Kardec 1996, 421F).

   Espiritistas contend that the spirit world is arranged in a hierarchy that places the Judeo-Christian creator at the top with a whole series of *seres* (beings), *espíritus* (spirits), *ángeles guardianes* (guardian angels), and *guías* (spirit guides) ranked below that encompass the entire spectrum of angels and seraphim, Catholic saints and holy personages (fig. 2.14), historical leaders, "bad" or "lesser" spirits such as demons, and lastly, the spirits of ordinary people who have crossed over to the world of the dead (fig. 2.15). The spirit guides most often encountered in ceremonies and represented in the religious folk art of botánicas are Africans (*negros* or *congos*; figs. 2.16, 2.17), Native Americans (*indios*; fig. 2.18), Gypsies (*gitanas*; fig. 2.19), and ascended masters such as the Buddha (fig. 2.20).

Espiritistas maintain that the spirits are able to interact with the living and, when contacted through a medium, can offer solutions to a variety of human needs: economic, emotional, medical, and social. A spiritual séance is one of the primary means by which mediums contact these ethereal beings on behalf of themselves and clients. The central feature of this rite is a table-altar—called a *bóveda* in Cuban tradition and a Mesa Blanca in Puerto Rican—usually covered with a white cloth and bearing candles, crystal clear vessels of water, works by Kardec, Bibles, flowers, scented colognes, and other ritual items. In creating these altars, emphasis is placed on establishing an atmosphere of clarity and purity that will allow divine entities with similar characteristics to be more readily channeled by the medium. The ceremonies are generally comprised of a litany of prayers and scriptural recitations meant to invoke the presence of spirits, followed by a period of trance-like discourse between the medium, the channeled beings, and other participants in the séance.

FOLK CATHOLICISM

Folk, or vernacular, Catholicism, as opposed to doctrinal church practice, refers to expressions of faith as actually practiced by believers. Such expression generally emerge out of everyday experience, or *lo cotidiano* (daily life). This widely shared religious heritage is a key cultural, historical, and ritual strand linking the specific rites and healing traditions supported by botánicas. Notable among material aspects of Latino vernacular religion are the personal use of saints' statues (*santos*) and ex-votos (*milagros*) and the building of home altars (*altarcitos*), yard shrines (*nichos*), and nativity scenes (*nacimientos*). The divinities or sanctified personages most often invoked are the Holy Family, the Archangel Michael, and blessed figures officially recognized by the Catholic Church, such as Saint Jude, Saint Francis, and Saint Martin. Frequently juxtaposed with these are other supernatural entities and sanctified individuals such as La Santísima Muerte (fig. 2.27), San Simón (fig. 2.25), and José Gregorio Hernández (fig. 2.29), personages who, although not officially authorized or sanctioned by the Catholic leadership, figure prominently in localized expressions of vernacular piety.

2.21
The divine patroness of Mexico and the most widely known and venerated incarnation of the Virgin Mary in the Americas, La Virgen de Guadalupe is arguably the central feature of Mexican and Mexican American Catholic worship. Envisioned as a protective mother figure, she is appealed to for a wide variety of needs. Accordingly, botánicas sell numerous candles, prayer cards, statues, and other devotional materials dedicated to her, and many feature shrines in her honor. Photograph by Patrick A. Polk, Botánica y Templo San Simón de los Llanos, Los Angeles, 2004.

2.22
This incarnation of Christ as Divino Niño Jesús is popular particularly among Mexican and Mexican Americans botánica owners and their clienteles. Several shops specialize in the sale and repair of infant statues used in Christmas manger scenes (*nacimientos*) and which are also frequently taken to church on January 6 to be blessed during the celebration of Epiphany or the Day of the Kings (El Día de Los Reyes). Photograph by Patrick A. Polk, Botánica Divino Niño Jesús, Huntington Park, 2004.

2.23
Also exceedingly commonplace are images of El Santo Niño de Atocha. Viewed by the Church as a true embodiment of the Christ Child, the Santo Niño de Atocha is widely venerated in Spain, Latin America, and, increasingly, the United States. Divine protector of children, prisoners, and migrants, he is usually depicted as an angelic adolescent with curly locks of hair and is dressed in pilgrim's garb. Photograph by Patrick A. Polk, Botánica Eleguá, Los Angeles, 2003.

HANDWRITTEN MESSAGES LEFT FOR SANTO NIÑO DE ATOCHA AT THE CHURCH OF OUR LADY OF ANGELS, OLVERA STREET, LOS ANGELES

Niño de Atocha, from my heart I ask you to help get rid of my problems at home. Give me peace. May things work out between my sons. I put myself in your hands Niño de Atocha.

Dear Niño, please heal Hannah. Give her a quick recovery. We leave her in your precious hands. Thank you.

Thank you Santo Niñito de Atocha for the life of this marvelous being [note attached to a photograph of an infant].

I thank you Santo Niño for illuminating my road so that I can be with my brothers and sisters and parents.

2.24
Saint Jude (San Judas or San Judas Tadeo), whose New Testament letter stresses that the faithful should persevere in harsh and difficult circumstances just as their forefathers did before them, is accordingly the patron of hopeless cases, desperate situations, and lost causes. Photograph by Patrick A. Polk, Botánica Angel de San Judas, Los Angeles, 1999.

VOTIVE CANDLES FOR SAN SIMÓN AND THEIR USES

RED	Love, fidelity, desire
YELLOW	Protection (for adults)
GREEN	Business and prosperity
BLUE	Employment and good fortune
PINK	Health and hope
BLACK	Protection from enemies and jealousy
BROWN	Protection from ill will and evil thoughts
LIGHT BLUE	Money, happiness, voyages, and education
WHITE	Protection (for children)

2.25
San Simón, the unofficial patron saint of Guatemala, is popularly described as a wealthy European (usually an Italian) visitor to Guatemala who provided food, medicine, and other goods to the indigenous Maya and was miraculously transformed into a saint. Typically he is shown seated in a chair with a cane or staff in his right hand. He usually wears a wide-brimmed, black hat and a white shirt, black suit, shoes or boots, and a red tie or bandana. A trickster-like figure who reportedly has a drinking problem, he is often invoked for treatment of addiction, assistance with immigration and other legal matters, and for matters of love and marital relationships. Photograph by Patrick A. Polk, Botánica Eleggua, Lynwood, 2003.

2.26
Juan Castillo Morales was, according to legend, a young Mexican soldier falsely accused of rape and summarily executed on February 17, 1938, in order to protect the real culprit, his commanding officer. As Juan Soldado, he is renowned as a divine victim-intercessor, and the shrine erected over his grave at Panteón Jardín No. 1, Tijuana, Baja California, has become a regional landmark. Although described by some worshipers as a helpful soul (*alma*) rather than a saint (*santo*), he is thought to be a protector of migrants (legal and illegal) and a guardian of the underclass, the young, and those mistreated by authorities, much like other saints of the United States/Mexico borderlands. Novena reproduced with permission of Calli Casa Editorial, Santa Ana.

2.27 (right)
A haunting, shrouded skeletal figure bearing a scythe, Santísima Muerte (Sacred Death) is considered by some to be the spiritual inverse of La Virgen de Guadalupe and, although perhaps ancient in origin, has become increasingly popular in the last two decades. One turns to Santísima Muerte for help with personal needs that might appear too unseemly to request of the nurturing mother figure of Mexican Catholicism. Known variously as La Santa Muerte (The Holy Death), La Niña Blanca (The White Girl), and La Flaca (The Skinny One), this personification of death is appealed to for protection from the dangers of contemporary life. Closely associated is the Guatemalan "Angel of Death," Rey Pascual. Photograph by Patrick A. Polk, Botánica La Madrina, Huntington Park, 2004.

2.28 (above)
Known as the "Angel of the Poor," Jesús Malverde was reputedly a Robin Hood-like bandit who stole from the rich and gave to the poor in and around Culiacán, the capital of the Mexican state of Sinaloa. He was executed in 1909. Some say his real name was Jesús Juárez Mazo, while others suggest that his legend is an amalgamation of the lives and violent ends of several local desperadoes. Viewed as a champion of the downtrodden, in recent years he has become associated with the cross-border drug trade and is occasionally referred to as a "*narco-santo*." Despite, or perhaps because of, his antiauthority persona, he is especially appealed to for justice, economic aid, and personal health and safety. Label reproduced with permission of Indio Products, Inc.

2.29
Born in Isnotú, Venezuela, in 1864, José Gregorio Hernández was trained as a physician in Caracas and Paris and received acclaim for dedication to the practice and teaching of medicine, as well as for his devotion to the poor and to charitable works. Hernández died tragically on June 29, 1919, when he was struck by an automobile while on the way to purchase medicine for an elderly and impoverished patient. Almost immediately following his death, tales of cures effected through his supernatural intervention began to multiply. Today he is considered a national folk hero, as evidenced by postage stamps printed in his honor, and the Catholic Church is currently considering him for canonization. Photograph by Patrick A. Polk, Botánica Eleggua, Lynwood, 1995.

FOLK PRAYER TO JOSÉ GREGORIO HERNÁNDEZ

Oh, my all-powerful Lord! You have brought your beloved servant José Gregorio to Your heart, and to whom, with Your great mercy, gave the power to heal the sick of this world. Give him, Lord, as Spiritual Physician, the grace to heal me, both in body and soul. I ask you this favor, Dear Lord, in the name of Your beloved Son who taught us to pray "Our Father who art in Heaven..."

Dear God, I am grateful for your healing blessings through your servant José Gregorio, to whom you gave the power to heal the sick of this world. Lord, by Your Grace, please grant him the divine power to help me heal both my body and soul. Lord, I pray that I may follow the example of José Gregorio in my life, and be a channel for humility, charity and loving kindness. Amen.

2.30
Known as the *curandero* of Los Olmos Ranch, near Corpus Christi, Texas, Don Pedrito Jaramillo (1829–1907) was born in Guadalajara, Mexico, and subsequently migrated to the United States. His healing abilities developed later in life, as he was fifty-two when he first started practice as a *curandero* in Texas. Tales of his curative powers, his piety, and his generosity have given him great repute and made him the object of faithful devotion even in death. Each year thousands of pilgrims and health-seekers visit his shrine near Falfurrias, Texas, leaving written requests for help, gifts of thanks, and votive candles among other things. Photograph by Don Cole.

CURANDERISMO

Integrating elements of popular Catholicism, Native American medicine, European magic and witchcraft beliefs, various metaphysical doctrines, and contemporary biomedicine, practitioners of Curanderismo (*curanderos* or *curanderas*) believe that the ability to heal is God-given and often claim that they began their medical practice as a result of divine calling. Traditionally, the healers worked out of their homes and tended principally to the needs of friends, relatives, and neighbors. As botánicas have become more popular and accepted institutions, however, many *curanderos* have set up shop outside of the home. *Curanderos* recognize illnesses and afflictions with both natural and supernatural causes. Remedies for physical and spiritual problems require prayer, spirit mediumship, and the utilizations of herbs, oils, holy water, and other sacred objects. A fundamental precept of Curanderismo is the idea that the patient must actively participate in his or her own treatment for it to be effective. Acting as a medical and spiritual advisor, the practitioner helps the patient to harness the healing power of God. Some *curanderas* and *curanderos* such as Don Pedrito Jaramillo (fig. 2.30), María Sabina (fig. 2.31), and Niño Fidencio (fig. 2.32) were widely acclaimed for their abilities during their lifetimes and following death emerged as spiritual guides, curative spirits, and supernatural protectors.

2.32
Niño Fidencio was born José Fidencio de Jesús Constantino Sintora in the Mexican state of Guanajuato at the turn of the twentieth century (either 1898 or 1900). He was orphaned at a young age, and following a visitation by Jesus Christ in the guise of a stranger, he soon manifested miraculous healing powers. He eventually established a spiritual hospital, attracting numerous acolytes and patients from all over the world, and following his death in 1938, he was transformed into a folk saint. Popular chromolithograph.

2.31
Acclaimed as a *curandera* and shaman, María Sabina (1896–1985) achieved great notoriety as the practitioner who introduced the sacred mushroom or Velada Ceremony to the eminent ethnomycologist R. Gordon Wasson. Wasson had visited her home in the tiny Oaxacan village of Huautla de Jiménez during his quest after the legendary hallucinogenic mushroom *teonanácatl*—said to have been used by the indigenous Mazatec peoples of the Mexican states of Oaxaca and Veracruz. Having discovered the properties of the plant as a youth, María Sabina became known as a healer and wise one (*sabia*) whose knowledge and skills were sought after by local residents as well as international visitors desirous of documenting (or experiencing) consciousness-altering rites (Wasson 1974).

CONCLUSION

The interplay of faith, ritual, and aesthetic creativity—typified by shrine building and altar making—is central to the spiritual and therapeutic systems encountered in botánicas and offers those who enter the possibility of meaningful, and sometimes life-changing, experiences. For both the faithful and those looking for a fulfilling faith, traditional images and understandings of divinities and the objects believed to be sacred to them help to focus hopes, needs, and desires. At the same time, traditional representations of the divine are increasingly infused with or filtered through the perspectives, rites, and symbols of other sacred traditions, expanded upon with images from American popular culture, and shaped and honed by the personal inclinations and aesthetics of individual practitioners. Shop owners and their clienteles routinely experiment with new ways of visualizing and experiencing the sacred, and this ongoing process of incorporation, reinterpretation, and innovation is what provides the religious folk art found in botánicas with much of its vitality. ❧

2.33
Black Christ of Esquipulas,
Guatemala, and Native
American spirits. Photograph
by Don Cole, Botánica
San Simón de los Llanos,
Los Angeles, 2004.

BOTÁNICAS

Sites of Healing and Community Support

Claudia J. Hernández and Michael Owen Jones

Herbal products for sale in the window of one of many botánicas where we conducted interviews might suggest that this is simply a naturopathic shop. Inside, however, sculptures of African warriors majestically flank the main aisle, prints of Native American healers decorate the walls, dense arrangements of colorful seven-day candles (*veladoras*) bedeck the countertop, and an altar for the Guatemalan folk saint San Simón—complete with offerings of alcohol, flowers, money, and food—sits on the floor in a corner behind the main display case.

The walls of the consultation room, situated immediately behind the sales area, are adorned with images of San Martín de Porres, San Lázaro, Santa Bárbara, and Mexican folk saint Jesús Malverde. An enormous altar fills a third of this consultation area. It features two tall wooden statues of Native American warriors adorned with feathers and rabbit fur, a pair of figurines of Mama Francisca and Negro José, Catholic statues of Santa Bárbara and Nuestra Señora de Misericordia (Our Lady of Mercy), and a seven-day candle depicting Jesús Malverde. A vase containing yellow and orange flowers stands on the left side of the altar, while another holding pink carnations sits on the right side. A small black cauldron with incense is placed near the center in front of a large glass goblet of clear water. A bottle of Florida Water and an egg, which are used in spiritual cleansings, also appear on the table. Clearly this is much more than a retail establishment dispensing homeopathic remedies. It is in fact a locus of the spiritual, and the abundant assortment of sacramental items so richly displayed reflects the needs of the community as well as the spiritual traditions of the owner.[1]

Proprietor Raul Martínez[2] notes that his store's religious affiliation is with Catholicism, Santería,

3.1
Soap labels. Reproduced with permission of Saydel, Inc., and Indio Products, Inc.

and Palo; however, he clarifies, "Before being a *santero*, I am an *espiritista* [Spiritist]. An *espiritista* is born an *espiritista*." Although Martínez divined people's problems as a child, it was not until he was eighteen that he began performing spiritual works and visiting botánicas. He recalls, "When I went to the botánica [it] was because I needed material, I needed to buy duck eggs that they don't sell in the store, I bought different candles that I couldn't find anywhere else, different herbs and incense that you use in [spiritual cleansings], in other words the material needed to do my job."

When Martínez began shopping at botánicas, he developed friendships with store owners who introduced him to their faith and thus helped him develop his spiritual abilities. As he explains, "I always looked younger than I am, and that was of intrigue to people because I would always buy things and know what I was buying, and I always paid them, and I never had to ask them what was good nor did I ask them for advice. I always got there and knew what I wanted, and that's when they began to talk to me about their beliefs and their religion."

At his botánica, Martínez sells sacramental items and herbal products and also reads tarot cards and cowries for his clientele. He offers spiritual cleansings as well. These can be as simple as rubbing flowers on the person's body or as elaborate as using candles, incense, and animal sacrifice along with prayer. He has significant knowledge of how to treat ailments, however, he notes, "What we mostly do is love issues, solutions as to love issues, to get love, to keep love, always some complication with love." He is also consulted about court cases, immigration problems, and alcoholism.

Like Martínez, many botánica owners are self- or community-designated healers, counselors, or consultants who ascertain the troubles of their clients through various techniques of divination and provide advice, *limpias*, referrals to doctors and clinics, and herbal or ritual therapies. A typical consultation (*consulta*) lasts an average of twenty minutes and costs between fifteen and twenty-five dollars.

Martínez usually initiates a session by having the client explain the nature of his or her problems. One young woman, for example, came to him hoping that he could determine whether bad luck or witchcraft was the source of her work-related troubles and failing health. She told Martínez that she had been sick for two months, she was not getting along with her peers at work, and a relative had said bad things about her. After listening attentively, Martínez shuffled his tarot cards, placed them in front of her, and asked her to divide them into three stacks and to pick one of these. Martínez then laid out the cards she selected and pointed to each one telling her what it meant. He determined that her misfortune was due to sorcery inflicted by her envious relative. He recommended a *limpia* to break the spell and ensure a prosperous future. Three weeks after this consultation and treatment, the woman had regained her health and received recognition for her efforts from her peers and her superiors.

Although some botánica proprietors focus on physical ailments, the majority attend to social and psychological ills. Healers often perceive problems as originating in "environmental sources." This blanket term may indicate such possible causes of stress as work or household responsibilities, problems relating to illegal immigration, injuries incurred on the job, and emotional distress produced by discrimination or from the cultural differences that have emerged between immigrant parents and their children.

Despite the fact that healers have varying theories of healing and different diagnostic approaches, some generalizations can be made about their beliefs and practices. Prominent among these is the notion that illness may result from supernatural as well as natural causes. Complaints originating in the latter realm are effectively dealt with utilizing home remedies, over-the-counter products, or prescribed pharmaceuticals. Weakness in one's soul or the influence of a malevolent entity is also thought to cause somatic or psychological symptoms to develop. Such causes are usually identified through divination and are treated with rituals, supplication to folk saints or spirit guides, and medicinal herbs.

Martínez relates that if a person believes a relative to have become alcoholic as the result of witchcraft,

> What they usually do is they walk through the streets where they know that people drink on the street, and if he's a beer drinker, they'll pick up a beer can, an empty beer can found on the street, and they'll put the person's photograph inside the beer can, and then they'll add other ingredients like mainly holy water and different types of oils, and just powders and organic ingredients [plant matter], and then they'll put it in front of the statue of San Simón, and alongside they will just light purple candles for domination so that the person will have the ability to dominate and overcome this problem of alcoholism. That is when they do it without the person knowing it. If the person drinks hard liquor they will find a small liquor bottle thrown on the street, and do the same spell.

Martínez adds, "The idea is for you to transfer that alcoholism to the other person that threw that bottle or can on the street and get rid of it."

LIMPIAS, OR RITUAL CLEANSINGS

In addition to treating clients with rituals of transference, practitioners often assist them with *limpias* aimed at getting rid of negative energy. The type of cleansing performed depends on the healer's religious orientation as well as on the client's particular needs. Simple *limpias* may be offered at no cost. Complex ones requiring the burning of copal incense, the use of perfumed water, oils, candles, and eggs, and extensive prayers and petitions may run from forty to fifty dollars.

A special *limpia* conducted for a woman by Juan Reyes, a Guatemalan *curandero* and botánica owner, to assure luck and protection throughout the year, required that the client's head and hands be wrapped in aluminum foil while she held candles of different colors. Dense smoke from burning copal enveloped her. Reyes took a swig of strong-scented Florida Water and spewed it on the client's head, face, and back; he then passed three fresh eggs over the woman to remove

3.2
Packaged herbal mixture used in spirit-cleansing baths (*limpias*). Reproduced with permission of Indio Products, Inc.

3.3
Homemade herbal baths blessed by the spirit of San Simón and distributed by a local botánica for ritual and medicinal use. Photograph by Michael Owen Jones, Los Angeles, 2000.

negative vibrations. He next patted her head, shoulders, and back with red and yellow flower petals to ensure success in love and good health, followed by rubbing a large crucifix on her head several times while praying to San Simón, to whom he is devoted, and chanting petitions on her behalf. The foil with which she had been wrapped was then removed. After this Reyes placed the candles that the woman had held on the floor, surrounding them with the flower petals and eggs (the latter, which had absorbed the "bad influences," were to be disposed of by the woman who was instructed to throw them over her shoulder in an empty lot after leaving the store).

SACRAMENTAL OBJECTS AND HERBAL REMEDIES

Botánicas carry an assortment of products used for therapeutic purposes, among them *veladoras*, oils, incense, bath preparations, and powders. Such items are purchased in an effort to secure luck, prosperity, and a variety of other benefits. Candles are highly specialized in function, and the inscriptions they bear or their color indicates the salubrious results that they may be used to achieve. Yellow, for example, assures good health, green attracts money, red guarantees love and affection, blue secures tranquility in the home, and black causes or reverses harm. Aerosol cans vividly decorated with saints, cats, Native Americans, African spirits, and other images indicate some of the needs compelling people to visit botánicas. They bear such designations as "Strong Luck" and "Good Fortune"; "Attract Money," "Win the Lottery," and "Fast Money" (*dinero rápido*); "Steady Work"; "Make Lover Return"; "Peaceful Home"; "Court Case" and "Just Judge"; "Cast

3.4
Blessing and spirit-invoking sprays displayed at Indio Products, Inc., an international wholesaler of ritual products based in Southern California. Photograph by Don Cole, Central Los Angeles, 2004

3.5
Oils, soaps, colognes, and other aromatic items used to heal, protect, and sacralize the body. Photograph by Don Cole, Indio Products, Inc., Central Los Angeles, 2004.

Off Evil"; "Protection from Envy" and "Keep Away Enemies"; and "All Purpose" (*para todo*). The contents are sprayed on a person, around the room, or at an altar.

Medicinal plants and products are also commonly sold. Some healers carry only a small number of prepackaged herbs, such as chamomile, rosemary, and mint. Others market vitamins and supplements commonly found at health food stores. Martín González, a Mexican *espiritista/curandero* who operates a botánica in Echo Park, specializes in the management of somatic complaints such as muscle pain, headaches, digestive disorders, minor wounds and burns, insomnia, fatigue, and upper respiratory infections. Approached by a woman seeking his help in dealing with migraines and sleeplessness, González asked her if she was under stress. He also inquired about when she experienced the pain, how often, and how long it lasted. The woman did not feel tense, but she did admit to working a lot. To ascertain whether or not her problem was supernatural in cause, González proceeded to read the woman's aura by first cleansing himself with Florida Water and then holding one of his hands in front and the other behind her head to feel her energy. He asked her to close her eyes while he chanted a prayer. After determining that the client was merely fatigued and experiencing nervous tension, González recommended that she run cool water on the back of her head where she felt the most pressure and that she drink valerian tea prepared with the skin of a green apple.

Among the medicinal plants grown by several herbal specialists in their yards or collected along city sidewalks and in vacant lots are *albahaca* (basil), *yerba buena* (spearmint), *epazote* (wormseed), and yucca. Others include *romero*

3.7
Friar Robert Lentz. *San Martín de Porres*, 1993. A saint celebrated for his healing abilities, San Martín de Porres is shown with containers of valerian (*valeriana*) and sage (*salvia*), sacred herbs reputed to have great curative powers and routinely utilized in folk remedies. Image © Robert Lentz, reproduced with permission of the artist; color reproduction from Bridge Building Images <www.BridgeBuilding.com>.

3.8
Herbs and medicinal plants grown at a botánica. These are used in baths (*limpias*) and in the preparation of topical remedies, such as oils or salves. They are also infused in teas. Photograph by Patrick A. Polk, Los Angeles, 2000.

3.6 (oposite)
Product labels. Reproduced with permission of Saydel, Inc., and Indio Products, Inc.

(rosemary), which is employed as an astringent; *sábila* (aloe) for burns; *ruda* (rue) to treat gastritis as well as to induce labor; papaya as an aid to digestion; *cola de caballo* (horsetail) for kidney stones and inflamed bladder; *floripondio* (angel's-trumpet) to treat arthritis and also to induce sleep when the flower is placed under one's pillow; *salvia* (sage) for bronchial ailments and for spiritual use; and *árnica*, or wolfsbane, which laboratory tests suggest is effective in reducing inflammation by stimulating the activity of white blood cells and dispersing fluids from bruised tissue.

Some botánica owners know the medicinal uses of dozens of plants. Most are familiar with a core of twenty-five to thirty. For colds, fevers, and bronchitis, healers recommend teas and baths of *eucalipto* (eucalyptus), *gordolobo* (mullein), *jengibre* (ginger), *té de limón* (lemongrass), *verbena* (vervain), and other aromatic plants. They suggest garlic as a treatment for infections and hypertension; *póleo* (pennyroyal) in the form of a tea to relieve indigestion and anxiety; *estafiate* (wormwood), as well as *epazote*, for gastrointestinal ailments; sweet basil and mint, among other herbs, to attend to insomnia and nervousness; macerated leaves of *llantén* (plantain) applied to wounds to reduce inflammation and a tea from the seeds of this plant to ease nausea; and *chayote* (vegetable pear) and the *tuna*, or fruit of the nopal cactus, as treatments for diabetes.

One *espiritista* recommends a tea made from rosemary to diminish *dolor de cabeza*, or headache pain. When asked how long it takes to work, he responds, "Well, there are people for whom the effect happens psychosomatically—upon drinking it, they feel better." Another treated a woman with migraines using

3.9
Carlos Meraz, an *espiritista* who has owned botánicas near MacArthur Park grows more than sixty plants in his yard for use in remedies and ceremonies. Photograph by Michael Owen Jones, Los Angeles, 2001.

3.10
Carlos Meraz gives a simple *limpia*, or cleansing, to each of his guests at a party honoring San Simón. Photograph by Michael Owen Jones, Los Angeles, 2001.

baths that contained salt, alcohol, and bellflower. "I don't know about people's faith, but I pray a lot for them and the pain goes away," he said. "People get ill from pressure, bad treatment, pollution, and the food is not organic" but laden with insecticides.

Some of the practitioners and their clients stress their use of unadulterated plant materials as natural remedies that, while they may work more slowly than prescription medications, have fewer adverse side effects and promote the body's ability to heal itself. "I don't ever remember going to the doctor as a child," said a Mexican American woman who has spent all of her seventy years in East Los Angeles and whose yard contains nearly fifty plants, about half of which are medicinal. "We always had the home remedies. Even today, I'll go to the doctor for what I think is the last resort, to tell you the truth. And I try to avoid any drugs or over-the-counter things as I've become knowledgeable [about plants]. When I was younger I would take anything [prescribed medication] that was supposedly for that ailment, but not anymore."

This woman emphasized her unwillingness to treat her seven children and herself with antibiotics unless absolutely necessary. She grows medicinal plants for upper-respiratory infections, anxiety, and gastrointestinal disorders. Numerous scientific publications indicate that commonly used herbs have pharmacologically active ingredients and consequences, for example, eucalyptus has antiseptic, expectorant, and astringent qualities, while chamomile has an antiseptic, anti-inflammatory, antispasmodic, and carminative effect. Rue contains over 110 chemical compounds, twenty-two of which have known biological activity, including anti-exudative, spasmolytic, abortifacient, and antimicrobial. Common mullein (*Verbascum thapsus* L., family Scrophulariaceae), which healers grow to treat inflammatory diseases, asthma, spasmodic coughs, and other pulmonary problems, has known antibacterial activity. Hence, the plant materials most frequently utilized by Latino herbalists may well be effective for the applications proposed.

———◆◆◆———

Botánicas provide a place for people to congregate, socialize, and discuss political and other issues without fear of censure or reprisals. Some sponsor festivals, parties, or religious ceremonies attended by families from the immediate communities but also from other cities. As sites of healing and communal support, botánicas operate not only as settings for spiritual contemplation but also as information bases. This is apparent to any visitor who sees that beliefs about illness and its treatment are passed down from healer to client and are also transmitted among patrons. Healers tend to folk ailments (e.g., *susto*, or "fright," and *empacho*, or "blocked intestine"), social ills (difficulty finding or keeping a lover, immigration and court problems, stress, depression, alcoholism, etc.), and supernatural matters. They can empathize with their clients, for many have suffered the same problems. They speak the same language, sharing not only regional dialects but cultural concepts and religious precepts. The practitioners who operate botánicas care for the whole person not just the client's symptoms, and they offer culturally appropriate recommendations for physical, psychological, and spiritual conditions.

Traditional practitioners associated with botánicas are younger and better educated than has been assumed for folk healers. Almost half of the forty-one practitioners in our sample are in their forties and fifties while a fourth are in their twenties and thirties. With regard to the twenty-eight people about whom we have this information, more than one-fourth attended high school, seven earned a bachelor's degree, and five went to graduate school. They would serve well as a bridge in efforts to develop community health care programs that link families with conventional medical practitioners who lack their native familiarity. Many botánica owners insist that they are willing to distribute information to clients about the prevention and treatment of sexually transmitted diseases and other health concerns, a desire that should be utilized in the health system. Recognizing their existence, exploring their contributions to the spiritual and health care of immigrants, and ultimately incorporating them more fully in developing policy initiatives and community health care programs will help maximize an already existing resource for many immigrants' spiritual and emotional needs, social problems, and physical ailments. ☙

"STIR IT UP"

An Elegba Throne by Felipe and Valeria García Villamil

Patrick Arthur Polk

Those who befriend Eshu[1] are not troubled by want of money;
Eshu, you are the one I'm going to befriend.
Those who befriend Eshu are not troubled by want of wives;
Eshu, you are the one I'm going to befriend.
Those who befriend Eshu are not troubled by want of children;
Eshu, you are the one I'm going to befriend.

IFÁ DIVINATION CHANT, CITED IN BASCOM (1969, 155)

Elegba[2] is a powerful thing, an incredible thing. He represents possibilities.

FELIPE GARCÍA VILLAMIL

"For us," proclaims Felipe García Villamil, renowned Afro-Cuban drummer, artist, and priest, "Elegba comes first in all ceremonies." Indeed, by rule, Santería, or Lucumí, rites open with prayers, chants, or drumbeats for the deity Elegba (Eleguá), and he receives sacramental offerings of food and drink before the other *orichas* or worshipers. This, however, does not mean that he is the chief divinity within the Santería pantheon; Obatalá, "the Creator" and father of the *orichas*, holds that position. Rather, this honor is largely due to Elegba's role as the divine messenger or spokesman (*vocero*) who facilitates communication between *orichas* and their adherents. If this connection fails, a rite will be unsuccessful. Thus, Elegba is a divine transistor broadcasting the desires of gods and humans across

4.1
Shrine or throne (*trono*) for the *oricha* Elegba fashioned by Felipe and Valeria García Villamil. Photograph by Don Cole, Los Angeles, 2004.

4.2
Felipe García Villamil stringing
an elaborate beaded necklace
(*collares de mazo*) for the *oricha*
Yemayá at his home in Central
Los Angeles. Photograph by
Patrick A. Polk, 2003.

4.3
Valeria García Villamil at a cele-
bration (*toque*) for the *oricha*
Obatalá. Photograph by Patrick
A. Polk, El Monte, 2004.

dimensions of the sacred and profane, making them mutually intelligible in the process. Not surprisingly, Elegba is also seen as the *oricha* who controls luck and destiny and is closely associated with divination and divinatory tools such as the cowries (*dilogún*) used to foretell events, discern the sources of problems, and prescribe ritual solutions.

Without looking up from the thick multistranded necklace (*collares de mazo*) he is fashioning, and pausing frequently as he alternately threads groupings of blue and clear crystal beads symbolizing the goddess Yemayá, Felipe outlines the essence of Elegba: "Elegba is the owner of the roads, the one that opens and closes them...he's the first to bring good and bad...for us Elegba is a figure like a playful child, but there is also the notion of a being that closes the roads when one doesn't act right or when one doesn't do things correctly." Felipe acknowledges that it would take a very long time to describe the characteristics and complexities of Elegba, or more specifically, his many incarnations (*caminos*). Like other *orichas*, Elegba has numerous avatars—some say 121 or more—each personifying a specific aspect of his basic attributes.

As the owner (*dueño*) of all literal and symbolic thresholds, crossroads, and pathways, Elegba can enable adherents to succeed by removing all obstacles, but he can also assure their failure by sealing off all avenues to success if he feels slighted or mistreated. A mischievous trickster figure conceptualized as a "knife that cuts both ways," he is always watching human actions, promptly rewarding proper behavior and even more quickly punishing misdeeds. Felipe's wife, Valeria, states: "He's that energy that will stir everything up if you ain't paying attention." In other words, Elegba makes sure that no ritual requirement or pragmatic aspect of daily life has been overlooked by adherents. If appropriate attention hasn't been paid to work, communal relationships, or family matters, Elegba becomes the devil in those details. At the same time, because his own faults, failings, and frailties are so well known, Elegba is considered the most human of the *orichas*.

SEEING ELEGBA

Divine Messenger do not confuse me.
Divine Messenger do not confuse me.
Let someone else be confused.
Turn my suffering around.
Give me the blessing of the calabash.

POPULAR PRAYER, WIDELY CIRCULATED ON THE INTERNET

Juoriwa [Elegba] *was carving cudgels;*
He used the cudgels to surpass everyone on earth.

DIVINATION CHANT, CITED IN BASCOM (1980, 671)

"Elegba likes to move around the house," Valeria replies when I ask why his altar is no longer stationed in the front room. The bead-encrusted gourd, bottle, and staves; the rustic goatskin bag; and the seven-day candle bearing the likeness of the Holy Child of Atocha have all been moved elsewhere (fig. 4.4). Even the

4.4
Atoyebi García Villamil's Elegba shrine. Photograph by Patrick A. Polk, Central Los Angeles, 2003.

concrete bust of Echú Ayé (see below) with its cowry-shell eyes and mouth—which always remains near the front of the house—has been moved to a small table next to the door. Valeria's matter-of-fact response highlights my misconception. I had interpreted this as a fairly static set of symbols used by practitioners to represent and perhaps invoke a divinity, but Valeria describes a conscious, active presence roaming about the home according to its own will. She explains that Elegba prefers to be "in the action," and for this reason, he is periodically transferred to the *cuarto de orichas* in rear of the house, especially on the occasion of ceremonies.

At the time of my query, the García Villamils were preparing a celebration (*toque*) for the *oricha* Oyá, which was being sponsored by a member of their religious family, or *ilé*. For this reason, they were erecting a throne (*trono*) in the back of the house, which was, at the time, the hub of spiritual activity. Constructed on special occasions such as initiations, initiation anniversaries, or "birthdays" (*cumpleaños*), as well as non-calendrical events such as when a practitioner wishes to thank a particular deity or set of deities for rendering aid in a time of need, thrones are temporary installations intended to present the *orichas* in all their glory. Complete with rich, and often expensive, draperies, lavish displays of fruit and confections,

4.5
Throne (*trono*) for Oyá in the home of Felipe and Valeria García Villamil. Photograph by Patrick A. Polk, 2004.

4.6
Elegba's *güiro*, created by Felipe and Valeria García Villamil. Photograph by Don Cole, Los Angeles, 2004.

and radiant bouquets of flowers, they highlight the presence of spirit. Although thrones are occasionally encountered in *botánicas*, they are primarily set up in the homes of practitioners and are the focal point of ceremonies.

The Elegba altar that moves throughout the García Villamil's South Los Angeles residence belongs to Atoyebi, the youngest of the couple's three sons. A teenager now, Atoyebi was crowned as a child of Elegba while still a toddler. Comprised primarily of sacramental objects created by Felipe and Valeria, the altar's centerpiece is a large cowry and bead-covered calabash (*güiro*) container in which several items representing Echú Ala Nike—the specific incarnation of Elegba that serves as Atoyebi's *cabecera*, or "the ruler of his head"—have been secreted. Felipe cut and shaped the calabash and then wrapped it in concentric circles of beads—red, black, white (Elegba's colors)—up to the base of its neck. From there, Valeria took over, covering the neck itself with a cascading array of cowries. This detail was her innovation, inspired by Yoruba artifacts on which cowries are featured more prominently than is generally the case in Afro-Cuban religious arts.

Although the *güiro* of Atoyebi's Elegba rests on a small wooden table, Felipe maintains that the ideal seat, or *odó* (as it is known in Yoruba), for Elegba would be a large piece of dark-colored granite or a similar hard rock (*piedra*), perhaps two and a half feet high and nearly as wide. Individuals spend a significant amount of time sitting on the *odó* as part of the initiatory ceremonies during which they are crowned. Elegba's *güiro* is normally draped with an elaborate necklace (*collares de mazo*) fashioned from beads in his colors. According to Valeria, this heavy, sash-like adornment is a symbol of prestige demonstrating during ceremonies that "you have the honor to wear the banner of the deity." Felipe adds that it also signifies that the person wearing it "has power, has magical secrets" and that the individual "received the energy of Elegba and was transformed a bit." Thus, in addition to imparting status, the *mazo* infuses a believer with the blessings and beneficence of the represented deity. Continuing with this theme, Felipe testifies that it defends initiates (*iyawós*) from negative influences at the time of their crowning. "It is a protection from their *oricha*, to save them from sickness, from jealousy."

Each major *oricha* has a unique ritual implement that serves as a paramount symbol and is prominently displayed on shrines and carried by adherents when possessed by that deity. Elegba's is the *garabato*, a hooked staff usually crafted from guava wood and decorated with red, black, and white paint or beads. Closely patterned after the simple wooden tool used by agricultural workers in clearing sugarcane of grass and weeds, Felipe maintains that it is "the force [Elegba uses]... to clear the thicket [*maleza*], it's for opening the paths, clearing away the trash, making the road ready for one to pass. Also to clear negative things from the road." In keeping with Elegba's additional role as divine enforcer and punisher of misdeeds, the *garabato* is also understood to be an instrument of misfortune. Felipe notes with a devilish laugh that the *oricha* can use his staff to "put stones in your way when you don't do the right things."

Concerning the origin of Elegba's *garabato*, Felipe relates the story (*pataki*) of how while traveling through a forest, Elegba, Ogún, and Ochosi—the trinity of masculine and protective *orichas* known collectively as "the Warriors" (Guererros)—arrived at a town that was in a state of crisis. One of the king's daughters had been kidnapped, and the ruler promised a great prize to whoever rescued her. The Guerreros tracked the princess to a cave where a dragon held her captive, and they slew the beast and returned the maiden. To each, the king offered the hand of one of his three daughters in marriage. But the three decided that they did not desire this reward. The grateful father then presented them with a set of surprise gifts. "To Elegba he gave the *garabato*, which was a sacred object in that town to clear the roads...to Ogún he gave the machete, and to Ochosi he gave the arrow." Reflecting the power ascribed to the *garabato*, Atoyebi's Elegba is usually equipped with at least three.

In keeping with his persona as a warrior and traveler, Elegba possesses a shoulder bag or *cartuchera* (lit., "cartridge pouch") crafted from goatskin and detailed with cowries and beads in which necessary supplies such as tobacco and favorite foods are kept. It also holds medicines and herbs needed "to clean the road, to clean people" and is used to store "the things that come" when Elegba is traveling back and forth to the four corners of the universe.

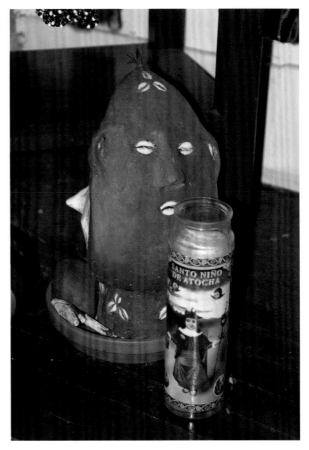

4.7
Elegba and fellow warriors (Guerreros) Ogún and Ochosi installed as part of a throne (*trono*) erected in honor of Ochún. Photograph by Patrick A. Polk, Central Los Angeles, 2003.

4.8
Echú Ayé, an avatar of Elegba, charged with protecting the front door of the García Villamil home and warding off danger. Photograph by Patrick A. Polk, Central Los Angeles, 2003.

Complementing the *cartuchera* is Elegba's *cantimplora*, a decorated flagon or canteen. Perhaps echoing the deity's martial aspects, the term *cantimplora* can also be translated as "powder flask." Felipe, however, clearly conceptualizes it as a container for consecrated liquids—preferably light rum or white wine—that quench the thirst of the *oricha* when he is on the move. Although Elegba enjoys drinking liquor, frequently asking for it when he possesses adherents, Valeria indicates that the rum in the *cantimplora* is really there to cool Elegba off through evaporation, much as cologne is used.

Resting on the floor in front of Elegba, is a large cement-filled conch known as Echú Ayé, the avatar of Elegba charged with guarding the front door of a home. Packed with herbs and other spiritually active items, it was hand-shaped by Felipe in the form of a face with cowry-shell eyes and mouth. A metal spike protrudes from the top of Echú Ayé's head representing the knife (*cuchilla*) he uses to protect and cut through problems, the plume (*pluma*) that signifies his royalty, and the phallus that is emblematic of his creative impulses. "Without that," Felipe asserts, "the Echú is not complete." When Atoyebi's Elegba moves to the back of the house, taking his *güiro*, *garabatos*, *cartuchera*, and *cantimplora* with him, Echú Ayé remains at the front door.

THANKSGIVING

Today I know this country better, I know where I'm standing, I know what I want and where I am going. I have had many problems, even with my family here, and I have made many mistakes, I lost my house, I lost my things. But this is my life and this is my family and I have learned to accept them.

FELIPE GARCÍA VILLAMIL, CITED IN VÉLEZ (2002, 166)

It took a while, but we hung in there. Sometimes you really have to know the value of what you have. Be able to see how the things that you do or the practices, what they really bring to you.

VALERIA GARCÍA VILLAMIL

Valeria recounts the circumstances of her initiation as a priestess of Oyá, the *oricha* who rules her head, and the simultaneous consecration of Atoyebi as a child of Elegba during the last week of November 1994. Felipe had just made his first trip back home to Cuba since leaving the island in 1980, a sojourn motivated by the fact that even after a decade, he was still finding it difficult to adjust to life in the U.S. Unfortunately, the Cuba of 1994 wasn't the place he remembered. Felipe was shocked by how much the country had deteriorated. Upon returning to New York, where the family was living at the time, Felipe became distraught, dispirited, and emotionally out of sorts. Valeria remembers, "We decided that the only way we could pull it together and keep him from just losing it would be to make an offering to Ogún." This is Felipe's ruling *oricha* and, therefore, the one considered best able to help him in times of need. At the close of the ritual that followed, it was discovered via divination that Atoyebi, then four years old, should be initiated as a child of Elegba for his protection and health.

This revelation did not surprise Valeria, who notes "[Atoyebi] was like a little old man when he was a child, very grounded, very sensible," alluding to the popular characterization of Elegba as a youth with a wizened face. This presented several significant problems however. First of all, initiations are quite expensive and require elaborate preparations. Shortly thereafter, seemingly by chance, someone came to Felipe and asked to be initiated as a priest of Ogún. Taking this as a heavenly sign, it was decided that Atoyebi would be crowned at the same time. Valeria herself, however, had yet to be crowned as a priestess of Oyá, and this presented a second dilemma as Felipe was adamant that a young child should not be initiated before his or her parent. Valeria explains, "If the parent is deceased that's one thing, but if the parent is living it can result in a spiritual imbalance between the parent and the child." And so it was decided that the mother and child would both "make their saints" together. Following the initiations, Felipe still struggled to come to terms with his separation from Cuba and his family there, but bit-by-bit things came together. Summing up Elegba's role in this development, Valeria states: "I think that you have to have some amount of upheaval or turmoil to keep things from getting stagnant because as soon as anything gets stagnant it stops to produce and reproduce. You have to have things stirred up and change, and you have to have struggle in your life in order to keep you honest and to keep you moving forward." She believes that these personal transformations helped to solidify their family situation and helped to maintain their relationships and shared identity through religious practices. Seeking better opportunities and a safer life for their children, Felipe and Valeria moved to Southern California in the late 1990s where they now live with their sons Ajamu, Miguel, and Atoyebi; their daughter, Tomasa; and their granddaughter, Divali.

CUENTAS

Beads were wealth when existence began.
DIVINATION CHANT, CITED IN BASCOM (1980, 471)

We use this place like a factory, no? This religion of ours is very concerned with money. We're not going to say we won't ask for anything if there is something to give, because we must buy things for the work. If we can help people with the things they come to this house for, we'll help them. We are going to do it with love and absolute responsibility.
FELIPE GARCÍA VILLAMIL

Sitting at his cluttered worktable in what would be a breakfast nook or laundry room in most other homes, Felipe picks up the frayed end of a white thread, wets it in his mouth, and then carefully aims it toward the eye of a long, thin silver needle. It takes a couple of tries to pass it through, but soon enough he's ready to affix more beads (*cuentas*) to the red cloth-covered sacramental *güiro* dedicated to the *oricha* Dadá, a divinity associated with vegetation, unborn children, money, and other symbols of creative potency. After carefully spearing several red *cuentas*, he sets them in place, and using a curved mattress needle, he then loops a second thread over the first firmly holding the ornaments in place. Switching back and forth, Felipe wraps line after line of beads around the exterior of the calabash.

Whether crafting sacramental pieces for his own family *orichas* or fulfilling commissions from other adherents, art collectors, or museums, Felipe sometimes works as many as twelve hours a day, measuring time by the strands of beads that encrust these sacred objects. Asked how he manages such time-consuming and detailed labor, he answers, "Patience. Lots of patience. And no time for television." At this moment, his granddaughter, Divali, who has been mischievously playing with Felipe's work materials, accidentally spills a bag of beads, sending tiny red orbs racing across the table and onto the floor. Felipe snaps at her, but soon enough she gets a smile and hug. And then back to work on the *güiro*.

It's nine thirty in the evening and Felipe is clearly tired. Dadá's *güiro* needs finishing. After that he has to fashion a smaller one for the Guerreros. He also has to make yet another *güiro* for Elegba and then four or five *collares de mazo*. "One for Changó," he counts, "one for Ogún, one for Yemayá,..." he trails off

4.9
Felipe García Villamil playing the batá drum during a ceremony for the *oricha* Oyá held at his home. The ornately beaded drum cover was made by Felipe. Photograph by Patrick A. Polk, Central Los Angeles, 2004.

4.10
Felipe García Villamil working on a bead-encrusted calabash (*güiro*) representing the "crown" of the *oricha* Dadá. Photograph by Patrick A. Polk, Central Los Angeles, 2003.

as the phone rings. Someone wants Felipe and his sons to drum for an event on Saturday. There's no way he can do it as he's already scheduled to play at other ceremonies the whole weekend. After hanging up, he wonders aloud how people can call up at the last minute expecting him to be available. Through the doorway behind Felipe, I can see his consecrated set of *batá* drums stored in their customary place in the *cuarto de orichas*. I marvel at how the same hands that deliver vigorous beats to the goatskin-covered double-heads of a *batá*, forcing the drum to loudly praise the gods, can also craft such ornate and seemingly delicate beadwork. When I leave around ten thirty, the TV is on in front of the house. The room is empty, however, except for Elegba and his compadres, Ogún and Ochosi, who had apparently decided, since the time of my last visit, that the action was now there. *Orichas* have that luxury. Sitting at his worktable, Felipe stretches, rubs his eyes, and keeps on beading. ✦

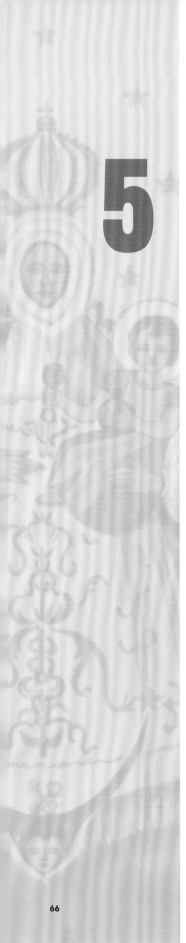

5

REMEMBERING AMÉRICA

A Powerful and *Cariñosa* Daughter of Yemayá and a *Maestra de las Ciencias Ocultas*

Yves Marton

¡Yemaya Olodo! Virgen de Regla ¡Qué Buena eres!
FROM THE SONG "PARA OCHUN"
BY HECTOR LAVOE AND WILLIE COLON

Cuando no hay cariño, no hay nada.
AMÉRICA LEYVA

Many academics writing about those who possess the spiritual and traditional knowledge that I associate with América Leyva—*santera*, *espiritista*, botánica owner, and my *madrina* (godmother or sponsor)—assume a stance of objective analysis, detached observation, cultural or religious advocacy, or postmodern—almost prurient—curiosity. I am in fact trained in anthropology, but this is not my primary concern here. The memories I present in this essay are of a personal, sentimental sort. They have little to do with exclusively cultural questions or with the investigation of belief systems from a fundamentally materialistic perspective, yet they linger vividly in my consciousness years after they occurred.

It is difficult to relate verbally what América Leyva taught me when so much of it was bound up with her extroverted Cuban sharing of a vivid energy and spirit (*ánimo*), a passion, a desire to give her all, a generosity coupled with exemplary behavior. The love and energy that a truly inspired and genuinely spiritually connected *madrina* can give to her *ahijados* (spiritually adopted followers, lit., "godchildren") is beyond comprehension, and it cannot be replicated.

5.1
Postcard representing La Virgen de Regla, an incarnation of the Virgin Mary recognized by practitioners of Santería as Yemayá, goddess of the ocean. Editorial Escudo de Oro, Barcelona.

It cannot be reduced to a formula. It cannot be memorized in a ritual. It cannot be passed down automatically through teaching, imitation, or blood. It is either there, or it is not.

An imposing and charismatic Cuban woman of African descent, América was born in Havana on September 26, 1926. Part of her deep respect for spiritual matters may have come from early personal experience. As a small child she had been severely ill and nearly died. Espiritismo (Spiritism) had proved the only thing capable of saving her life. Thus she viewed her spiritual path as a matter of life or death, rather than something to be considered at leisure in the same way one might regard a collection of dead butterflies.

For many years América operated Botánica Oggun, which is now run by her daughter, and at one point she owned another botánica in Culver City. Dried herbs, other natural substances, *estampas* (small printed prayers to specific saints), candles, oil, and colognes could be obtained there. She also had herbs growing in the front yard of her house, which she would sometimes pick and give directly to her *ahijados*. Most of the major rituals América performed, which could last from a few hours to several days, were carried out in her home or at the residence of someone working for her. Smaller rituals that were accessible to many people were sometimes carried out in the botánica. América seemed to enjoy being in her home. The botánica seemed more like a business to me than the place where she had in-depth interaction with her *ahijados*. It also served as a place of contact and meeting. If one wanted to locate América, the botánica was the place to go to find her whereabouts. The significance of the botánica was made clear as we escorted América's coffin to its resting place. After leaving the church, the funeral cortege followed a convoluted route so that it would pass in front of and encircle the botánica on the way to the cemetery.

América's utterances were frequently terse and aimed at the essence of things. She once told me, "Echa pa'lante lo demás es bobería! Son momentos no más" (Move forward [in your life], the rest is nonsense. It is only passing moments.)[1] Another time, she remarked, "Lo bueno de esta religión es que limpia a uno" (The good thing about this religion is that it cleans you [spiritually]), and with those few words she clarified so much about Santería and its path. Her succinct statement stands in marked contrast to the mystification of these beliefs promoted by some members of the younger generation and by a number of ambitious leaders and self-appointed spokespeople. América was critical of some of the people who wrote about or spoke in public concerning Santería or the Lucumí tradition even at that time, over twelve years ago. "[For] those who know, it is a very simple thing," she remarked, "And those who don't know speak a lot, write a lot.... they create a lot of problems."

América was a daughter of Yemayá, the embodiment of motherhood, someone who cares for her children and protects them, who motivates and encourages them to do well, to push themselves to achieve in life. Her love is infinite and her wisdom is without boundaries. She knows today what will happen tomorrow. The slights, ingratitude, and betrayal of her children and of others hurt her deeply. In flesh and in spirit, América was indeed an embodiment of Yemayá.

FIRST ENCOUNTER

I first heard of América Leyva from a close friend who had accompanied a young Latin American anthropologist desirous of a reading from her. América had told the anthropologist the identity of his "head" *oricha*—an identity he seemingly disputed—and informed him as well that his mother was in danger. Although he apparently dismissed the entire reading, within a few days, the young anthropologist received an urgent long-distance telephone call informing him that his mother had fallen seriously ill.

I initially visited América for a reading at her home in Hawthorne in the fall of 1985. She exuded an aura of warmth and authority, and when she welcomed me with "Entra mi hijo" (Enter, my son), her strong voice seemed to completely fill the room. My life at the time seemed to have reached a dead end. I was ill at ease but could not determine why. I had recurring nightmares that disturbed my sleep, and I felt excessively dependent on people. I was very anxious about my health and energy. I had experienced a sudden and marked weight loss, had digestive problems, and suffered from constant exhaustion. My family was very concerned about me, and although I visited medical doctors, they could not determine what was wrong with me.

América told me, "Naciste para ser cabeza no para ser cola" (You were born to be the head, not the tail). This seemed to be the exact opposite of my situation at the time, but it gave me encouragement, hope. She further declared, "¡No seas esclavo de nadie!" (Don't be anyone's slave). These words echoed with significance for me. She also correctly noted (without any prompting from me) that I had recently experienced health problems and had lost a significant amount of weight. But more surprising yet, in the middle of the divination, she accurately diagnosed a very specific symptom that I had noticed. América had absolutely no prior information about my health, and I had not shared the details of the specific symptom she remarked upon with anyone.

She also accurately described the general state of my life, making certain remarks and predictions about my future that were not to be realized for another five years. These predictions were made in somewhat metaphorical terms, and she spoke of the *orichas* as symbolic of dynamics in my life. She told me that I was involved in situations that were deleterious to my psychological and physical health. She recounted a particularly memorable story about the *oricha* Changó, saying "as Changó is a good Catholic, he cannot kill" but that he was acting or fighting to protect me in a specific situation. As I understood it, I needed to be careful because Changó could only do so much, he could not "kill."[2] I needed to do my part.

América also told me at this first meeting, "Soy maestra de las ciencias ocultas" (I am a master of the occult sciences). She continued, "Yes, I live in this little house like a nobody, while doctors have hospitals, money and power, but I can cure people. And often when the doctor cannot do anything, I can. I have cured many diseases. I have saved the lives of people whom they could not help." As I later came to realize, this was indeed true.

During this reading, she also spoke to me about values and behavior modification. She told me to avoid drugs and alcohol and to be very careful about my

5.2
Mexican chromolithograph of
the Virgen de Regla.

diet, avoiding red meat and canned and fried food. She also recommended that I refrain from arbitrary sexual encounters. Regarding my family, my mother, and my girlfriend, she advised me to be patient and tolerant, to avoid being critical of little events or habits and to let minor upsets pass.

This was the first and only reading I ever received from América. She told me that she did not want to do additional readings once she knew a person, because the information she now had could mix in with the information she would be receiving spiritually. She was very serious about the need to be cautious and to avoid mixing imagination and previously known information with spiritual divination readings. Several years later América sent me for a reading with an *ahijada* of hers who worked at the botánica América owned for a time in Culver City. América instructed me to not mention that I knew her or that I knew anything about Santería, so that the reading would be more pure. This concern with veracity, validity, and reality was quite unique, and it was one of the common threads that I found among certain Cuban and Brazilian mediums. Their concerns bridged the space between the powerful traditions they were born into and an approach that might be characterized as scientific or as a form of non-elite empiricism.

I felt impressed by the precise diagnosis of my physical symptoms in América's reading, and her strength and encouragement invigorated me and gave me new optimism. She suggested that I come back and recommended that I undergo a type of cleansing called a *rompimiento*, which she described as being good for my health, energy, and *camino* (spiritual path). I later returned to América's house to undergo this cleansing ritual, bringing a change of new white clothing as instructed. After the ritual was over, I came out of the room clad in my new white attire, feeling calm, clean, refreshed, and very light. América was sitting in a large armchair. She gave me or perhaps had her *oyubona* (assistant) give me *los collares*, the sacred necklaces of the *orichas*. América then said to me, "You are now part of this house [group]. Anything [you need], if you are hungry, if you need something, you can always come here. This is your house [your home])." I was surprised to find that I had just become a member of a group.[3] I had not been told that the cleansing implied this. Nonetheless, I felt good with my new lighter energy. At that time, when Santería was still much more underground than it is now, América advised me to wear my necklaces under my clothes. She didn't want me to run into trouble with my family or others.

América vividly described this new energy I felt—and which people began to perceive in and around me: "Dios es un atmósfera alrededor del ser humano, es como una nube que te rodea" (God is an atmosphere around the human being, it's like a cloud that surrounds you). Indeed it seemed from the reactions of people around me—including those who knew nothing about what I had done—that this "cloud," the spiritual atmosphere surrounding me had been changed in a positive fashion. Within the ensuing months, I gradually regained hope, *ánimo*, strength, energy, health, and life.

Aside from the ritual prescriptions and protocol that América guided me through, our interactions often took the form of regular brief conversations. She put herself at the disposal of her numerous *ahijados*, and each time you talked to her, you felt as if she focused completely on the issues you brought. She was constantly active and appeared to sleep little. Her house was a hub of activity. If a ritual was not being carried out or godchildren weren't being oriented, then the furniture was being moved and renovations were in progress. Even late at night she would sit in her large reclining armchair by the telephone. Her *ahijados* would call, and she would pick up the phone and give them advice and encouragement.

I used to count on her in those days, and she would advise me to stay in touch regularly. One time during a particularly stressful period, I got in a car accident and called her past midnight. Sure enough, she was right next to the phone and picked it up immediately, advising me to keep my cool and telling me that it was merely a difficult period that I was going through. There was no irritability in her voice or any indication that I was importuning her.

At times América would make spontaneous statements that took me completely by surprise. Her short and seemingly offhand utterances hit things exactly on the mark and made me realize that she was speaking from a place of knowing. While to someone else these remarks might seem totally insignificant, at the moment she uttered them and relative to my state at the time, they were potent with meaning and power. One time I called América feeling confident in myself because I had made a special effort to organize my day and had proceeded to accomplish what I needed to do in an efficient and calm manner. I felt as if I were getting "on top of things." No sooner had she picked up the phone than she told me, "You're doing well today, that's how you must do it every day; you see how well things go when you just do your part, when you do [your best]!" I had not said anything to her about how my day had been going or my newfound organizational ability or my feelings about my productivity. My immediate internal response to her comments was "How did she know?" I remember once, after such a call, writing down "Is this América or is this Yemayá?" She seemed to know without my telling her how my health was faring, what my personal habits were, and how people treated me. Simply put, these were psychic occurrences that communicated their divine origin through their uncanny accurateness and timing. It was the presence of the *oricha* speaking to me through América. Again, on the surface these statements were ordinary and would never convince a skeptical outsider, but experiencing them repeatedly at perfectly timed moments and considering them in retrospect, I have no doubt that these were utterances coming from the all-knowing source, which may be referred to in different traditions as "spirits" or "*orichas*" or "God."

5.3
Brazilian chromolithograph of the icon variously referred to as Stella Maris, Mary Star of the Sea, La Diosa Del Mar, Iemanja, Yẹmọja, and Yemayá.

América conveyed much wisdom, love, *cariño*,[4] and common sense in her words. In contrast with some of today's practitioners, her emphasis was on helping and encouraging people and keeping matters as simple and truthful as possible. She had an instinctive rejection of all forms of mystification and exploitation of the religion and of spiritual matters in general. She said to me that she was not so prone to carrying out ceremonies as "nowadays" (i.e., in the 1980s) the *oricha* did not come down in as authentic and powerful a manner as when she was young. "When I was young, you could see Changó come down and take over an elderly woman and she would get all this energy and go as far as climb[ing] a tree with *el santo montado!* An old woman climbing a tree, running up a tree! Because that's how it was back then, the *oricha* had power. It was for real."

She took her knowledge and memory of genuine spiritual authority and phenomena very seriously. She described to me how in one instance two men came to her house, saying that one of them was possessed by the *oricha* Changó. She believed that the man was faking. This, in addition to involving dishonesty, was an affront to the religion and to her in her own home. She went to the kitchen and proceeded to boil oil or water, brought the pot to the man who was apparently possessed, and poured it down his back. The man screamed in agony, was burned, and left the house immediately. América explained that when Changó truly possessed someone that individual would become temporarily immune to fire and hot liquids.[5]

América was someone who might be called in Spanish "*brava*." She would not suffer abuse from anyone and was fearless, brave, and uncompromising. She did not allow anyone to lord it over her, even the police, and once refused to stop her car when they attempted to pull her over, because she knew she was in the right. "When we finally stopped the police asked us why we did not stop earlier. I said that we had done nothing wrong! And they had no reason to stop us!"

Although she valued being powerful and using the tools of the dominant society (money, possessions) to gain a position, América always maintained a respect and solidarity with poor people and never adopted an elitist approach to her followers. She treated people well regardless of their social or religious status.

One of the first things América told me had to do with her high valorization of plants, nature and animals, and her low overall evaluation of human beings:

> Plants are beautiful. Doctors take plants and by making drugs out of them they are able to take advantage of about thirty percent of a plant's usefulness. We use the whole plant, all of its juice, and we get a hundred percent. Plants are good for so many things. They can cure so many things. Nature has everything in it, but you have to know how to use it. Animals are beautiful too. They can be very intelligent,

much more intelligent than human beings. A dog, for example, can be very intelligent. From a distance, and without seeing him, a dog can perceive a human being's presence and predisposition. Human beings are part of nature, of course, but.... Human beings are full of vanity, they are full of egoism. Plants don't have any egoism. They are beautiful. [Marton 1986]

One time I asked her if she had a spiritual guide, like the Brazilian medium I knew who was guided by an African spirit who had formerly been a slave. She responded, "Yes, look over there," and pointed to a portrait an old Cuban lady of African descent with a white kerchief on her head and a serious demeanor. América explained that it was this spirit (*muerta*) who spoke to her.

América passed away very suddenly a few days after Christmas of 1992. Her death was attributed to diabetes and kidney problems, which had been worsening over the previous years. I felt her sudden absence acutely and mourned the disappearance of a strong, compassionate, and supportive friend. América disappeared from the physical world, but she reappeared to me, albeit on very rare occasions, in dreams, endowed with the same energy she had demonstrated in life. In one such dream she advised me to value what I had received from her, as well as from Afro-Brazilian religion. She told me to remember how my life had been saved by her and, by implication, all of the forms of knowledge related to her African-rooted tradition. Some time before she passed away, she referred me to a Cuban Spiritist for a reading, and the last time I spoke to her she gave me instructions that had to do with Spiritist practice. Indeed América's view of spiritual knowledge and tradition was very broad and valued other practices in addition to Santería and African tradition. In her view all of the mediumistic practices were tied to each other.

Everyone has a miracle, a gift inside. América had the gift of love, of compassion, of enthusiasm, but it was not locked inside. She shared it with everyone that she could. She had a deep and genuine connection to the spirit world and was a mixture of fierce conviction, confidence, warmth, and humility. She was, like other very special people, completely and utterly irreplaceable.

6

TRAVELS WITH CHARLEY AND MANUEL

Donald J. Cosentino

Por mi hermano, Manuel

Charley Guelperin is a Los Angeles *santero* who describes his religious calling in ways relevant to the spirituality of the City of Angels, "I believe I'm a warlock or a witch; a man in touch with nature, in touch with the cosmic world, with the astro world, and with the world of the Dead."

Manuel is Charley's spiritual father. He was born a king in the Congo five hundred years ago but was brought in slavery to Cuba where he fathered more than a hundred children. Charley was one of those children and somehow escaped his responsibility to become a *santero* back then. Now Manuel has come back to make sure Charley fulfills his destiny.

I have known Charley and Manuel for more than a decade. They've been occasional lecturers in courses I teach at UCLA. And for the last few years the three of us have been engaged in intense conversations regarding a book I'm writing about the Dead in African Atlantic religions. Our conversations have taken place at Manuel's botánica in Hollywood; on travels to Cuba and Haiti; at Charley's country house in Las Vegas; and en route to these various places.

The following are extracts from those conversations, which I've arranged like "snapshots" in a photo album: "Charley in Buenos Aires"; "Manuel in Rio"; "A Greenwich Village Apparition"; "An Exploding Cauldron in L.A." As developed by Charley, these images illuminate his long and intense relationship with Manuel and the function of the ritual objects he's agreed to lend to the Fowler Museum for exhibition.

6.1
Statue of Manuel in the front window of Botánica El Congo Manuel. Photograph by Don Cole, Los Angeles, 2004.

But caveat emptor: stories conjured from such images can never be complete or balanced. Some shots are candid while others may be staged. But in either case, the snapshots are epiphanies, glimpses into the lives of their brilliant subjects. Readers may also reprove the earthiness of the language they encounter. But Charley and Manuel talk as they are—a priest and a spirit at home on the streets of L.A. (where many of us talk like that). The Judeo-Christian deity may speak in "thous" and "shalts," but divine discourse in Afro-Atlantis is looser, funkier, closer to the ground.

PROLOGUE: DON'T CRY FOR ME ARGENTINA

Argentines detest the mediocre and fear to be thought mediocre.
v.s. naipaul (1980, 124–125)

It's been said in the readings that the night I was born lightning hit in Buenos Aires. And in the light of the lightning, Manuel was fused to my mother's ovum.
CHARLEY GUELPERIN IN CONVERSATION, HOLLYWOOD

As he tells it, Charley Guelperin's life is as operatic as the gods he serves or the city where he was born—on a dark and stormy night. First son of German-Basque Argentines named Adam and Eve Guelperin, Charley was, on another plane, the last of the 121 sons fathered by Manuel, King of the Congo, who came crashing down from the lightning-streaked skies onto one of the great stage sets of history. As Evita sobbed "Don't Cry for Me, Argentina" from the balcony of the Casa Rosada, little Charley Guelperin would mingle among her adoring crowds below, hawking photos of the Peróns riding their palominos.

But you must widen the lens to gauge properly the whole gaudy scene. This is also the city of Jorge Luis Borges whose devious *Ficciones* are not so different from the tales told by Charley, who read to the blind old poet each afternoon after German school. This is the city too of Manuel Puig, where small town hustlers dream of being *Betrayed by Rita Hayworth*, or by *The Kiss of the Spider Woman*. It is the city of Harrods and tea at 5:00 and especially of the tango, fashionably appropriated from the bordellos down by the river where it was danced when Buenos Aires was a colored city too. But no more. Argentina is the land of the missing *negrito* and the missing *indio*—the Indians dispelled and the Blacks driven north, across the Río Plata and into "South America." No place was left for Manuel, King of the Congo, except through the technology of Espiritismo (Spiritism), which, by the age of Perón, had become the unofficial national religion:

> The Argentine middle-class...is swept by the new enthusiastic cult of espiritismo, a purely native affair of mediums and mass trances and miraculous cures, which claims the patronage of Jesus Christ and Mahatma Gandhi. The espiritista mediums heal by passing on intangible beneficent "fluids." They believe in reincarnation and the

perfectability of the spirit. They say that purgatory and hell exist now, on earth, and that man's only hope is to be born on a more evolved planet. Their goal is that life, in a "definitive" disembodied world, where only superior spirits congregate. [Naipaul 1980, 111]

6.2
Charley in his consulting room at Botánica El Congo Manuel. Photograph by Donald J. Cosentino, Los Angeles, 2003.

Espiritistas constitute a modern wizardry, describing their craft through an appropriated "scientese" (Charley frequently peppers his discourse with terms like "binary combinations" or "supernova"). This was Argentina's "New Age," and Charley grew up in the middle of it. "My grandmother started the lineage of spiritualism in my family. Then it succeeded to my Aunt Miriam, my Aunt Angel, my mother—who is a real Spiritist—and then to me. I'm the one who broke the mold because I'm the first male who actually practiced Espiritismo. Everyone else was female in my family. But I am gay, so maybe it's okay." While Charley now has many religious identities, it is important to remember which is primary, as he often asserts, "I became a *santero*, but I was born an *espiritista*."

Charley's "shining" was confirmed at the age of eleven when the ghost of Aunt Miriam materialized in his bedroom. After that, he had daily visits from "millions of spirits" (just like the kid actor in *The Sixth Sense*—one of Charley's favorite movies—who said, "I see them *all* the time"). Charley's spiritual skills developed quickly: "Hearing and channeling, clairvoyance and automatic writing. I was going into trance, falling on the floor shaking, foaming at the mouth." He was taken to all kinds of doctors until his mother said, "Quit wasting time...the kid is just coming of age spiritually." So he became a student at the Escuela Científica Basilio, established in Buenos Aires in 1917 to teach the technologies of Allan Kardec, the founder of modern Spiritism.

In a city that hungered for the occult, Charley had star quality. While other kids were riding bikes or playing soccer, he was busy doing readings or channeling spirits, including Gandhi, for lines of clients that stretched around the block. But one spirit remained lurking in the shadows. "When Manuel starting coming to me in Buenos Aires, everybody dismissed him. They didn't want to have anything to do with a Black spirit. And I wasn't aware of him consciously." But even then, there were intimations. Once at a Seventh Day Adventist Youth Camp, Charley was overcome while singing near a campfire. He leapt around the flames, burping and howling while the other kids cowered. The next day he was accused of "devil possession" and sent back home alone. "I never felt so lonely," Charley says of this early manifestation of a spirit who would reveal himself more fully on Charley's first visit to "South America."

BRIGADOON

*How I get to Brazil? When I was a teenager, I got a job in the
PR division of Walt Disney, with the movies he done with animals.
Because I always been involved with animals. I played a talking
basset hound named Socrates who made political commentary for
a radio show called* Five Minutes with My Dog. *I once owned a pet
shop which sold only white animals. I won the Argentine equivalent
of the* Sixty-Four Thousand Dollar Question *by answering a question
about dogs.*

CHARLEY GUELPERIN IN CONVERSATION, LAS VEGAS

Thus Charley found himself tramping the streets of Rio de Janeiro in a lion suit,
part of the advance team promoting Disney's *The Jungle Book*. On his day off, he
wandered into a *terreiro*, a temple for the spirits of Candomblé. As he tells it,

All of a sudden I heard drums coming from this house. And there
were seventy-five or eighty Black people there, dressed in beautiful
white gowns with necklaces. It was almost like a ghostly scene to
me. And they were playing drums and dancing in this trance, and
I was mesmerized by this scene. Immediately I went into a trance
and was mounted by Manuel. Well, Manuel found home. And for
the next eleven hours he danced and drink and smoke to make up
all those years he been waiting for this.

When I finally wake up, the next morning, all these Black
people were laughing. There was this man sitting on a throne, a
hunchback, dressed all in red, with a sword. He touched me with
the sword, the way a king would knight somebody. I was very scared
he would chop my head off. But he said to everyone, "Don't laugh.
He's a child of the spirits, and he has a mission to accomplish." So
he said to me, "Child, go in peace. Your mission is started."

So I left there, wandered down the shanty to the Copacabana
Hotel where all the Disney people were freaking out because I supposed to do a TV presentation in one hour. The next day I tried to
take myself back to the *terreiro*, but I was never able to find it again.

So like the fog-shrouded Scottish village in the musical *Brigadoon*, the
world of Manuel vanished. And for many years thereafter, Charley was left to
wander alone on this material plane: scooping coins from the Fontana Trevi,
working on a kibbutz in Israel, hitting the hippie trail to India, Vietnam in time
for Tet, Ashrams, Shinto temples. Charley kept popping up Zelig-like during
all the great scenes of the 60s and 70s. His penultimate adventure was with the
mob in Greenwich Village where he was working at Pennyfeathers and the Blue
Angel during skirmishes of the "Banana Wars."

And then Charley experienced his second sighting of Brigadoon. He was coming out of the West Village subway stop in Sheridan Square in December 1979.

It was snowing. I came out of the subway into the Village, and the whole world disappeared. I actually saw an ocean. I could hear the sound of the waves. And I saw myself sitting on the beach with my back to the ocean. In front of me was a bonfire. And behind the bonfire were eight little flames, like gaslights. Eight of them, and then they disappeared. The whole image disappeared. I walked four blocks to my apartment. Packed eleven suitcases and my dog and put a sign on the door saying, "Keep it all." Then I left for Los Angeles. Never been in Los Angeles before. Never knew anybody in Los Angeles.

Of course he had to make some quick excuses to his *padrone* for this hasty exit. But Charley never doubted the significance of the vision. Here was a theophany, choreographed by Manuel. Those were visions of Obatalá, Yemayá, and the other *oricha* gathered on the beach in Santa Monica, California. That's where he was being summoned. Manuel had come out of the shadows and would be with Charley forever.

TWO LOCOS AND A WARLOCK

> *I've been offered to open on Rodeo Drive, in Paris, in Milan. But Manuel doesn't want to move from Santa Monica Boulevard. I have to learn to be humble, he says, and that's why Manuel keeps me here. Well, whadda more humble place to be in but Santa Monica and Wilton? You have sometimes five Mercedes Benz and two BMWs parked outside—they come to see me between La Pizza Loca and La Pupusa Loca—between two locos! The Three Stooges, right!*
>
> CHARLEY GUELPERIN IN CONVERSATION, HOLLYWOOD

Charley's adventures in L.A. are of the type that church historians call providential. Revelations, manifestations, crossroad conjunctions, all orchestrated by Manuel. Through a chance encounter at a gay bar, Charley was introduced to Miguel Martínez, a Cuban *santero* who also had a Congo spirit, Jacinto. At their first meeting Jacinto and Manuel hit it off. As Charley recalls, "Now I'm in a dirt room. Fully dressed in a three-piece suit, with a beautiful shirt and beautiful jewelry, and now I am mounted. And I'm rolling around the ground, fully dressed, and there went my suit.... Manuel and Jacinto drinking *chamba* together, having a great time, and then I wake up and I'm a mess."

Martínez initiated Charley as a *santero* with the crown of Obatalá, creator *oricha* of the Yoruba pantheon. Charley's initiation name is Babafunke, "Father of the Anvil," since Obatalá promised to re-forge his new spiritual child like a hammer at the anvil. Charley's identity as Babafunke is separate from his identity as Manuel's 121st son; but that is another tale for another time. At Charley's *itá* (initiation divination), the shells warned, "two kings cannot sit on one throne," and two months later, Martínez was dead. So Manuel stepped into the breach. "I'm initiated," Charley says, "but I don't know nothing about the tradition. And I lost my teacher. And that's when Manuel took his place and really started to teach me. And really came the daily relationship with Manuel. He taught me to read the shells—the actual readings with the *ebós* and how to 'splain to people— was all Manuel's doing."

Manuel inhabits Charley's third eye and rides him like a horse at séances and ceremonies, revealing to others things he chooses not to tell Charley himself. Manuel is also physically present in a cauldron (*nganga* or *prenda*) full of sticks, bones, and objects of power that radiate Congo magic. Charley now keeps Manuel's cauldron in the basement of his house in Las Vegas, but during his poorer days, he kept it on the balcony of a rented place in L.A. The tale of that cauldron illustrates the intimate, though by no means easy, relationship between the spirit and the man (see box, p. 81).

Now for more than a decade, Charley and Manuel have run Botánica El Congo Manuel as a joint enterprise. The strip mall location is also providential. The botánica is indeed sandwiched between those twin "Locos," but it is also down the street from Paramount Studios, and from the chic plots (Valentino! Cecil B. DeMille!) of Hollywood Forever Cemetery (the inspiration for HBO's *Six Feet Under*). And just a few blocks north is Hollywood Boulevard, where blow job queens hustle Evangelistas for the lost souls.

It is from this world of L.A. Noir that Charley and Manuel draw their clientele: Paramount hangers-on, NBA stars, taxi drivers with "Migra" problems, homeboys on the run, transvestite hookers with erection issues, Israeli tycoons desperate to close deals, TV reporters on "Sweeps Week" assignment, professors soliciting hot book material, museum curators pitching hot shows. And what do they get for their money? (For a lot of money changes hands at the botánica.) They get spiritual readings that suggest new ways out of old dilemmas. They get therapies for sicknesses physicians can't cure. They get talismans that block enemies and open up energy fields. They get charms and bones for their own cauldrons and initiations into esoteric cults, but most importantly, they get compassionate and effective counsel from a five-hundred-year-old Congo bodhisattva manifested through the body of his immensely sophisticated and psychically gifted son.

Charley knows who brings in the clients. It is Manuel, installed in the front window of the botánica next to his wife, Francisca, who trolls the boulevard for new clients (fig. 6.1). Charley bought the statues of the two Congo spirits in Miami and delivered them to the cemetery for their initiation into the cult of the dead (Palo). There they received head *rogaciones* (ritual dressings) and *raimientos* (ritual cuts). Three animals were sacrificed to them. They were dressed in blessed beads and blessed clothes. Even their stools were baptized. There is nothing ersatz about these statues. They are alive with *aché* (divine energy). Their transport from the botánica to the Fowler Museum for the exhibition that accompanies this publication will be a religious procession, and their reinstallation will sacralize a secular space.

THE MIRACLE OF THE FLAMING CAULDRON

6.3
Putting the saint to work. In Catholic folk practice, statues and images of holy figures are sometimes inverted as a means of "speeding up" their intercession. An image of Saint Anthony, for example, may be turned on its head by individuals seeking to find a marriage partner, while statues of Saint Joseph are often buried upside down in the front yards of homes the owners wish to sell in a hurry. Coercion is sometimes more effective than prayer.

I kept the cauldron of Manuel on the balcony of my town house. But I was so irritated with him because I was broke, didn't have the money to pay for the town house. So I went out to the cauldron, in broad daylight, three in the afternoon, and said, "Listen, Motherfucker. If this is what you want, fine. But you better do something, because I plan to move into my car." Then I started to insult the cauldron. I said "I plan to take out my dick and piss on you." That's the biggest insult you can make to a cauldron. But I've never been known to be too polite.

So I walked away from the cauldron. I slammed the balcony door so hard it shattered the glass. My mother, father, and dog were all shivering in the corner of the room like I had gone mad. Then the cauldron caught fire! There were no candles, no fire anywhere, it just combusted. Flames were coming out of the cauldron, and the door bell rang. There was this tiny little lady standing there, and I'm shouting, "Whaddya want?" The old lady jumps three feet in the air and didn't know what to do, run away or what. So she says, "I would like to have a reading." "Come in!" I shout at her. She comes in, I close the door, and the bell rings again. Another person standing there. At the end of the day, I have $2,850. So I pay my bills and become a working spiritualist and santero.

When Charley was queried about the propriety of cursing at and peeing on his father, mentor, and best friend, he replied:

Are you kidding me? I tell the motherfucking nigger to come back from Africa. He's on vacation. He better get his shit together and come back to work on Santa Monica Boulevard.... He always complain about the way I talk to him. But he talks that way, and I'm a splinter of that same tree. Whaddya expect? If I come from a bonsai tree to be a refrigerator? You talk to me that way; I talk to you that way. But what would be considered by some people my disrespect for Manuel, actually is that I adore Manuel.

Most, if not all, *espiritistas* can recount a defining instance, often occurring during a moment of self-doubt or a crisis of faith, when the extraordinary abilities of their guiding spirits were demonstrated to them in an unmistakable and miraculous fashion. Although the abuse Charley heaps on Manuel in the episode Charley relates above may seem sacrilegious, such profanity, threats, and accusations of abandonment are a hallmark of many interchanges between Spiritist mediums and their otherworldly helpers. Some spirits more than others need to hear how desperately their aid is needed and must be informed of this in the very same manner—polite or impolite—by which they give advice to the living. —ed.

6.4
Bóveda at Botánica El Congo
Manuel. Photograph by Don
Cole, Los Angeles, 2004.

If Manuel and Francisca reign in the store window, they enjoy a considerably more modest status on the *bóveda*, which Charley maintains in the middle room of the botánica (fig. 6.4). *Bóvedas* are Spiritist altars, shaped like wedding cakes, each tier honoring a different "commission" of spirits. The arrangement is hierarchical, with a crucifix on top, representing the supreme teacher and most evolved spirit, Jesus of Nazareth. But Charley has affixed a red feather to the crucifix, signaling that it has been "crowned" by Olofi (see fig. 2.7), a *camino* (spiritual aspect) of Obatalá. That red feather further marks the syncretism Charley has introduced into religious practices inherited from female relatives, finding correlates for various of their spirits among the Afro-Latin *oricha*.

"The *bóveda* is the focal point of my life," Charley explains:

The top glass represents Olofi. The second belongs to Saint Claire, patron of spirits and all *espiritistas*. That's why there's an egg in the water. The third one represents my personal spirit guide who is a Native American, named Red Feather. And here are the spirits that used to belong to the Church. One is named María de la Cruz, a Spanish nun. Then there is the medical commission: spirits who work in the healing process for humanity. Then there is a step for my family...all the relatives that precede me here. And here is a picture of Lalo, who initiated me in Espiritismo at the Escuela Científica Basilio. And here is Saint Paul of Judea, who was also a doctor. He works with a commission called the Silver Wing Healer Society of London. Here's Rosita, and all the spirits who practice witchcraft and necromancy. The fourth one represents Manuel and the African commission of Congos.

As Charley descends the tiers, the spirits become heavier, more earthbound. He moves from the pure light of Olofi to the fleshiness of the Congos and finally to the inert world of bones. Hidden at the bottom of the *bóveda*, behind a lacy skirt, is the skeleton of a manatee. This is the realm of Olokun, goddess of the primal seas, which oozed out first life and enfold all the dead. And so the homologue is complete. The *bóveda* circles from alpha to omega. From womb to tomb. From Olofi to Olokun—and back again.

Of all the vehicles for Manuel's physical manifestation: the plaster statue, the cauldron, the *bóveda*—the most powerful and revealing is the body of Charley himself, the horse that Manuel rides during séances. I have seen the manifestation often enough to recognize its telltale signs. Charley's head lowers. He burps. His leg stiffens. Someone rushes over to take off his shoes and roll up his pants legs. Someone else fills his calabash with rum. His bare foot curls into an excruciating arc, evidence of the torture Manuel suffered five hundred years ago. His laugh sounds piratical, something picked up from the pirates of the Caribbean? "I am ugly. I am Black. I have a fucked-up leg. But my heart is pure," he says in between laughing, crotch rubbing, rum swigging, and stubbing cigars out on his tongue (*¡saabrooooosoooo!*). Thus "Manuelito" embraces and teases his children, who seem to love him as much for his reprobate ways as for his sage advice.

Manuel's departure is even more abrupt than his arrival. While his children raise their arms and sing "Buenos noches," Charley rises from his chair, projecting himself toward them like a rocket ship. No matter the ceremony, Manuel leaves (like Cinderella) before the last stroke of midnight. But his departure can also signal the arrival of his dog, Chacho, Manuel's dark alter ego, who sometimes circles Charley's house after midnight, visible like a dark nimbus. It was Chacho who led Charley to Forest Lawn Cemetery when he crowned Ánima Sola, the spirit of the Suffering Dead. Chacho then deserted Charley, leaving him naked and too dazed to find his parked car. In this parlous state Charley had to hitchhike home from Forest Lawn, hiding his private parts with a dead man's bone.

6.5
Obatalá enthroned in the upstairs study at Casa Obatalá. Photograph by Donald J. Cosentino, Las Vegas, 2002.

6.6
A sepia portrait of Charley's Aunt Miriam at Casa Obatalá. Photograph by Donald J. Cosentino, Las Vegas, 2002.

EPILOGUE: LEAVING LAS VEGAS

I love my religion. It's a religion that doesn't apologize for itself. I don't hide myself behind a cross or a star. I am human. As a human, I am imperfect. My job in the religion is to fix myself. Nobody will do it for me. I have to do it for myself. And that's what Santería teach me to do. You fuck it up, you fix it. Period. Amen.

CHARLEY GUELPERIN IN CONVERSATION, LAS VEGAS

After a particularly hard personal stretch a decade ago, Charley decided to leave L.A. He bought a ranch style house in Las Vegas, dedicating it to Obatalá with hopes that the cool *oricha* would help him gather clients in a hot town. It didn't work out. "No herbs grown in the desert" Charley says, explaining why he couldn't maintain a *botánica* in Vegas. So he headed back to L.A., leaving his mother Eve with his long-time companion, also named Charley, to keep the ranch house as a kind of desert retreat for his *orichas* and himself.

A bronze plaque on the front door of Charley's house reads "Casa Obatalá." And indeed, from his satin throne in the upstairs study (fig. 6.5), the "White Oricha" rules over an eclectic crew of supporting spirits. A cigar store Red Feather guards the front door, while brother Green Feather attends the fireplace. A sepia portrait of Aunt Miriam, looking as glamorous as Rita Hayworth, is propped on a tripod in the dining room (fig. 6.6). The Gypsy Rosita ("that *puta*" as Manuel calls her) lurks in the shadow of the stairwell.

6.7
Charley's *bóveda* at Casa
Obatalá. Photograph by Donald
J. Cosentino, Las Vegas, 2002.

6.8
Portrait of Jacinto, Miguel
Martínez's Congo spirit, at Casa
Obatalá. Photograph by Donald
J. Cosentino, Las Vegas, 2002.

Appropriately enough, the basement is given over to the dead. Three
bóvedas are set up: two for the Charleys and one for mother Eve (fig. 6.7).
Between the *bóvedas* are three portraits. In the middle is Jesus, crowned with
thorns, the most evolved of spirits. To his right and left, like the good and bad
thieves on Calvary, are commissioned portraits of Jacinto, Martínez's mild-man-
nered Congo spirit (fig. 6.8), and grizzled Manuel (fig. 6.9), a Black man sitting
in front of his *palenque* (forest house) somewhere in Santa Clara, Cuba (where
his bones still remain hidden). Surrounding Manuel is his familiar iconography:
seven bolts of lightning streaking his sperm to Buenos Aires; his broken slave
chain replaced by a hissing snake; the warrior *oricha*, Changó, manifest in a
crouching tiger; and the tools of his trade: the skull, the machete, and most
important, the cauldron bristling with *palos* (sticks) and bones.

Across from the *bóvedas*, in a closed-off garage space, Manuel's material
cauldron is set up on a patch of yellow earth (fig. 6.10). When I ask if Manuel
minds being consigned to the basement, Charley assures me that he is perfectly
happy hanging around downstairs. He understands that the upstairs belongs to
Obatalá, represented by a cloth monkey hanging from a rafter above the cauldron.
A full metal coat of armor, sacred to the Palo warrior spirit Sarabanda, stands near
a rack of knives and swords mounted on the wall. All these martial implements
guard a cauldron bristling with its own weaponry: *palos* and bones incongruously
topped by a pineapple. To one side of the cauldron a black candle burns, on
the other a motorcycle helmet is set. (Charley tells me the helmet is being kept
enthralled to the cauldron, checkmating its owner who is in jail).

6.9
Portrait of Manuel, King of
the Congo, Casa Obatalá.
Photograph by Donald J.
Cosentino, Las Vegas, 2002.

6.10
Manuel's cauldron in the
carport of Casa Obatalá.
Photograph by Donald J.
Cosentino, Las Vegas, 2002.

Later, when I ask Manuel if he wishes his own bones were installed in the cauldron, he answers with real indignation:

I don't want my bones in an *nganga*. I was a slave one time, and I am not going to be twice. I am *egun* [spirit of the dead]. *Mayordomo*. I have a dog. I am not anyone's dog. I mount my horse, no one mounts me. If I were in an *nganga*, they would mount me. I would have to go where I was ordered to go. I was ordered when I was on earth, and I cut my chains. I was a king, son of Bangoche. I wasn't born to be the dog to no one. Not while I was on earth, and not while I'm a spirit. I have my *nganga*, but I have my dog under the *nganga*. It's a spirit named Chacho who is my dog. If I am king, I can't be servant. I am Bangoche. I can't be a servant.

Charley and I drove back from Vegas to L.A. listening to the melancholy, impossibly sexy tangos of Piazzolla. "These tangos tell my whole life," Charley said, with a wistfulness I hadn't heard before in his voice. The spiritual traveler is ready to move on. After Eve dies, he wants to chuck it all. Close the botánica, sell the house, get an RV, and drive around the country as an itinerant *espiritista-santero*. Put all the L.A. and Vegas *orichas* into cold storage, except for Obatalá and Yemayá who get packed into the luggage compartment. Manuel of course will be co-pilot. Together he and Charley will drive off to Davenport for readings, or to Fargo for head *rogaciones*. Hippy *espiritista* and Congo bodhisattva driving off into the sunset.

And then, perhaps, to meet Olofi?

The *orichas* taught me to be a king on earth and to be a heavenly king when I pass on. When you crown, you not coming back here. I want to move on. I've done this trip seventeen times, as far as I know. So it's long enough. I did a lot of shit in this plane already. Enough is enough. And I have somebody who patiently wait for me 400 years. That is Manuel. I cannot condemn Manuel to keep waiting for me. (Not that I want to die tomorrow, because I want to be 110, but when it's over, it's over.) I want to grab Manuel by the arm and say, "Let's take a walk nigger. Let's see what's happening out there. Let's go meet Obatalá face to face. Look how the old man looks."

And if Obatalá decides that I am able, ready, and deserving to meet God, let's go and see. I hope I don't shit when I meet him. If I ever see him I will probably shit on myself. He's not this old man sitting in a chair looking like Zeus imparting laws. No he's not. He's a creative force. Probably a monstrous image of exploding energy and creative force. Like a nova. Who the fuck wants to see a nova face-to-face? Maybe I want to see it in a show in the observatory at Griffith Park, but I don't want to be close to a nova when the thing explodes. So I'm content meeting with Manuel and Obatalá and just being up there with the pantheon. Walking with the guys and just seeing what they do from there. ⇐

"CANDLES, FLOWERS, AND PERFUME"

Puerto Rican Spiritism on the Move

Ysamur Flores-Peña

To Dorothy whose faith in the spirits inspired this essay

Espiritismo (Spiritism), also known as Mesa Blanca, is the official folk religion of Puerto Rico. It is practiced by those who adhere as well to new Afro-Cuban religions[1] and by those who refuse to dilute it. Spiritism arrived in Puerto Rico in the nineteenth century, traveling from France via Spain. In the Spanish colonies this new doctrine was initially embraced by the upper classes as a means of resisting the colonial government and the Catholic Church that supported it.[2] Gradually trickling down to the rest of the population, it mixed with other, more-established folk practices. Thus new spirits and forces joined its pantheon.

In the Spiritist séances, or *veladas*, held by the upper classes the most frequent heavenly visitors were scholars, illustrious politicians, and religious figures from history. Once Espiritismo hit the streets, however, mediums began to give voice to indigenous, African, East Indian, Chinese, Gypsy, Samaritan, and other spirits, including historically significant European figures. Thus the practice began to reflect Puerto Rico's racial composition (see appendix, p. 97).

Puerto Rican *veladas* follow a very specific pattern. They begin with the recitation of prayers from Allan Kardec's *Colección de oraciones escogidas* (*Collection of Selected Prayers*) and his *Evangelio según el Espiritismo* (*Gospel According to Spiritism*). These books, along with the Bible, reside permanently on the altar. After the prayers the "religious" spirits (those who were members of the Church, i.e., priests, nuns, and so forth) will manifest to counsel and preach. They represent God,

7.1
Puerto Rican Spiritist or Mesa Blanca altar arranged by Ysamur Flores-Peña. Photograph by Don Cole, Los Angeles, 2004.

7.2
Statues of a stereotypical male African spirit, often referred to generically as Negro José, displayed at Saydel Inc., a major wholesaler of Santería-related products. Photograph by Patrick A. Polk, Huntington Park, 1994.

and this is the reason for their appearance. It is after these manifestations, however, that the true genius of Espiritismo becomes evident. The spirits of the Indians follow; because they are considered the true owners of the land, they precede any other spiritual line.[3] These spirits are wise and skilled in the art of herbal healing. Because of their stature, almost every practitioner will count an Indian as a spiritual protector. The phrase "To' el mundo tiene un indio" (Everyone has an Indian) attests to their significance in Puerto Rican identity. After the Indians come the Africans generically identified as "Congos." The African spirits are fierce and abhor sorcery. Their warrior-like nature justifies their association with cutlasses, spears, and axes. The Indians and Africans will speak in broken Spanish, or *bozal*. The rest of the séance is open to the spirits of other races.

The composition of the altar and séance reflect the history of the region. The religious performances of the different manifestations parallel the migration patterns, allowing spirits to descend into the temple in the same order that they arrived in the Caribbean. By ritually codifying history, the Spiritist séance gave presence to groups who lacked a voice in society. It is true that Indians had also put in appearances at the séances of the elite, but their presence there alluded to the Romantic notion of the noble savage. In the popular devotions of the people, all races came to share heaven. Europe, in the eyes of the mediums, no longer held sway in the arena of salvation.

For practitioners this notion of the equality of the spirits was extended to the idea of cultural identity. The cultural perception of Puerto Ricans as the offspring of three mixed races was supported through the popular practice of Spiritism. Espoused by nineteenth-century Romantics, this ideal would never have found favor with the general public if it had not been visibly enacted in

7.3
Images of Jesus Christ and Native American spirits displayed near the Cuban-style Spiritist altar (*bóveda*) of Oscar Martínez a prominent botánica owner in Los Angeles. Photograph by Patrick A. Polk, Botánica Obatalá, Los Angeles, 2004.

7.4
Detail of an altar for the Madamas featuring traditional doll, statue, and offerings designed by Ysamur and Dorothy Flores-Peña. Photograph by Don Cole, 2004.

séances and temples around the island. In 1955 the newly created Instituto de Cultura Puertorriqueña presented the three races on its official seal, representing them as having equal status.[4] This philosophy crystallized the way in which Puerto Ricans viewed themselves in the cultural continuum of "la Hispanidad." The pantheon of spirits continues to evolve and is constantly admitting new denizens. True to the faith's egalitarian focus, all spirits bring with them their own personalities and cultural values. They remain true to themselves even though they must conform to the values of Christianity as understood by practitioners.

One particular line of spirits, however, stands outside the "norm." These African spirits take the form of wise old house slaves. Puerto Ricans call the female spirits of this line "Madamas"; and the males, "Madamos."[5] Although they, too, speak *bozal*, these spirits are distinct from the Congos or other African spirits. They are a sort of "bridge" between the pure African spirits and Creole spirits. A trip to any local botánica reveals the iconography of the spirits of this line. The Madamas wear a distinctive head wrap, always knotted in the front, and full skirts. Their garments are often plain white, but red, gingham, and polka dots are just as common. The Madamos are dressed in white and also wear a head wrap. As with the Indians, many practitioners claim one or more of these African spirits as spiritual guides.[6] Madamas are very wise, expert in herbal lore, and famous for bringing good luck to their followers. In Puerto Rico a Black doll dressed in the stereotypical guise of the household slave may be found gracing many altars and living rooms in honor of the Madamas.[7]

Although French is not widely known in Puerto Rico, the word *Madamas* is folk Spanish for the French term *madame.* I remember that my late mother Ana M. Peña, herself a Spiritist, used to call any female from the Virgin Islands

7.5
Mesa Blanca temple of the
Flores-Peña spiritual family.
Photograph by Patrick A. Polk,
Los Angeles, 2003.

Madamas. Could it be then that the French-speaking Caribbean provided the raw material for the creation of this character? After all, the broken Spanish spoken by these spirits seems to betray a foreign origin. Much to the dismay of the Spanish governor, many French families came to settle in Puerto Rico as a result of the Haitian Revolution. The Napoleonic invasion of Spain in 1808 also made French a fashionable language among the Spanish and Creole elites, to the extent that they were referred to as *afrancesados* (Francophiles). It also resulted in the independence of many Spanish colonies in the Western Hemisphere. In two Puerto Rican dances of African derivation—the Bomba performed in Loíza Aldea, the most African of Puerto Rican towns, and the Plena danced in Ponce to the south—women wear outfits that are very reminiscent of the way in which the Madamas dress. The question remains, however, who inspired whom?

The altar setting for the Madamas is standard in form and content. The main icon is a doll, usually made of cloth and dressed in the colors favored by the spirit. The characteristic head tie identifies the figure as a Madama. A basket of herbs, oils, and lotions is also part of the assemblage. Mediums use these dry herbs to make infusions and also add them to incense to heighten the power of their preparations. Madamas can treat both health- and spirit-related maladies, and their ability to exorcise evil spirits is proverbial. The "otherness" of these spirits is represented through color choice. Puerto Rican Spiritism is also known as Mesa Blanca (lit., "white table"), after the table around which mediums sit to work. Everything in the sacred space is white. Madamas with their often vibrant clothing and bandanas contrast with the cool atmosphere created by the use of white in the altar space. Nowhere else is the foreign personality of the Madamas more evident, however, than in the trance. Most spirits that manifest in the séance do not require any paraphernalia. In the case of the Madamas, however, the mediums tie their own head wraps with the knots in the front, "Madama style," and then out comes the basket, the broom, or any other ritualized element present at the altar.

Madamas are familiar with the world of the living and the world of the spirits. Because of their ability to negotiate the unknown, they seem best equipped to facilitate relocation and travel. The massive Puerto Rican migration to New York between 1948 and 1950 brought the Madamas to the United States. It was in New York that the first recording of Spiritist sacred music were made in the late 1950s. Records such as "Homenaje a la Madama" and singers such as El Madamo Joe are familiar to many Puerto Ricans in the U.S. and on the island. At about the same time, broadside prayers to these spirits appeared, and many began to carry them in their wallets to ensure success, protection, and happiness in the new environment. In the 1970s Chucho Avellanet, a popular Puerto Rican singer, recorded a Christmas song called "El paquete" in which a Puerto Rican immigrant instructs a friend on the island to go and see "la Madama Lula" and beseech her to alleviate his problems in the great city. In the late 1970s another pop singer, Dany Rivera, recorded a song titled "Jesús, María y José" describing a séance where a Madamo comes to provide counsel and healing.

Madamas are still the most beloved icon of Puerto Rican Spiritist practice, accompanying immigrants to new lands and assisting them in new endeavors. Popular artists in the United States created a new icon to represent them, the Seven Madama Powers (Siete Potencias Madamas). The main figure in this group holds a book, and six minor figures sit around her as if awaiting instructions. The stereotypical representation of Madamas does not conform to the notion of Puerto Ricans as a people. These spirits stand outside the discourse of race and identity by retaining their foreign speech and aesthetic. They straddle two realms and have become powerful because of their "otherness." In a new land that had to be understood, Madamas provided Puerto Ricans with reassurance and a link to their island and history. The Madamas also evolved with this new community; the Spanish divination cards, herbs, oils, and bright colors remained, but a new item, the book, became the center of their power. Possibly French-inspired, Puerto Rican by adoption, they are now set to become the teachers of their people. They have provided counsel to many generations, and it is only logical for them to show the way out of isolation through the most powerful of weapons, education. Who knows, Madamas may finally force Puerto Ricans to answer the question "¿Y tú abuela dónde está?" (Where is your grandmother?). Looking at the Madamas, we know that behind every one of us Ricans, despite our skin color, there is a Black grandmother.

LOS ANGELES 2004

When considering Mesa Blanca in Los Angeles, a number of questions come to the fore: (1) How does the practice survive in an area where Puerto Ricans are not culturally dominant? (2) Is Mesa Blanca flexible enough to accommodate other influences and still remain true to the social, religious, and cultural ideals it espouses? (3) What happens when the practice comes face to face with individuals from other spiritual and religious traditions whose vision of the spiritual work may contradict the philosophy of Mesa Blanca? As "exotic" religious practices proliferate in North America, every vernacular practice potentially becomes a new revelation to be added to those that came before it.

As a child I grew up in a "traditional" Puerto Rican household. My mother, a healer, had a very busy practice healing and counseling. She was my first teacher. To her I owe my first lessons in herbalism and the philosophy behind the practice that will dominate and guide my life for years to come. It was she who explained to me the different lines of spirits, their powers, and how to work with them. After finishing the training she could give me, she took me to another *espiritista* who would not only train me as a medium but also organize my spiritual cadre by identifying all the spirits by names and missions.[8] After receiving this information, I set up my altar.

The altar is both a personal expression of the spiritual cadre and a testament to personal and collective histories. As the medium progresses in his or her career, other spirits will join the cadre and by extension the altar. Icons of personal devotions and the individual devotions of the spiritual guides will become a veritable portrait of the individual's heavenly helpers. If the medium works for others, however, the altar becomes the collective property of those who come for help. The altar then is a liminal space in which the medium's personal history and that of the community served merge. Not only the spirits who work and frequent the altar are represented, other spirits will come to share this, the most democratic of heavens, as well. Deceased family members, friends, souls in need of prayer or a restful place can and will be given permission to enter this space. Pictures, personal possessions, symbols, and any object that may house the spirit's essence can find a place in the altar.

Marriage is not only a merging of personalities and properties but also of spirits. According to Spiritist belief every human being has spiritual guides and protectors, therefore the establishment of a household also entails the union of spiritual forces. For example, a couple may decide (if allowed

7.6
Detail of the Mesa Blanca altar in figure 7.5. Photograph by Patrick A. Polk, Los Angeles, 2003.

by the spirits) to establish an altar for the household. In another possible scenario, each spouse will keep an individual altar, but some icons will migrate from one altar to the other. Because of this, many mediums not only get married in the church but also marry in the spirit. The latter is considered the stronger union since those getting married are the two cadres of the spouses. This union is truly unbreakable.[9]

I came to Los Angeles in 1983, and I had been practicing Mesa Blanca since the time I was nine. I established my house not only as a Spiritist but also as a priest of Ochún.[10] My altar was thus enriched by the diverse population that came to my house: Mexicans, Central Americans, Asians, African Americans, Middle Easterners, and Caucasians. My altar now houses symbols drawn from Mexican and Central American Catholicism, Islam, Judaism, and any other faith that has significance for those I serve. When I married my wife, Dorothy L. Flores, icons from her Venezuelan spiritual practice also came to reside on the altar, especially the most important icon of Venezuelan Spiritism, María Lionza.

My wife brought her own altar, but icons from our separate altars were exchanged immediately. This act sanctified and legitimized our union in the eyes of the spirits. Today in our son's altar there are icons from both our altars. In this

7.7
Crucifix and water bowl (*fuente*), focal points of the Mesa Blanca séance. Photograph by Patrick A. Polk, Los Angeles, 2003.

7.8
Ysamur and Dorothy Flores-Peña
at Turey Spiritual Shop in
Hollywood. Photograph by
Patrick A. Polk, 1989.

way a spiritual succession becomes manifest visually by the use of icons and what I call the "language of placement."[11] Despite the complexity of these altars and their underlying hypotheses, I always remember the words of a very wise *espiritista* when I marveled at the simplicity of his altar when compared to others. His explanation was very humbling, and to this day I remember it: "Espiritismo," he said, "is candles, flowers, and perfume; the rest is decoration."

After twenty-two years in Los Angeles my altar is not the one I came here with. It has grown, thanks to the gifts of those individuals who have adopted it as their own, and many pictures of dead friends, godchildren, and relatives of those who come to the house form a permanent encampment. Different individuals also want their particular devotions to "live" with us. Does this mean that the altar has become less Puerto Rican? I think not. In spirit, if not in iconography, the altar remains true to the ideals of Mesa Blanca. It has given voice to diverse spiritual forces regardless of their origins. It was this ideal that gave rise to the doctrine originally and remains true to it. By encompassing so many spirits, the work of the medium touches more lives. ❦

7.9
Detail of the altar at Turey Spiritual Shop featuring images of Our Lady of San Juan de los Lagos and an icon of an East Indian spirit. Photograph by Patrick A. Polk, Hollywood, 1989.

APPENDIX: THE PUERTO RICAN SPIRITUAL CADRE

The spirits in a Puerto Rican séance, or *velada*, appear in an order that reflects patterns of immigration to the island:

- Indians
- Religious spirits or spirits related to Europe
- Africans or Congos
    - Madamas and Madamos (related to but distinct from Congos)
- Arabs
- Chinese
- East Indians
- All other spirits, including the Samaritan woman from the Bible and Gypsies

This spiritual cadre is under the direction of a Main Spirit, or Jefe del Cuadro, usually a saint of the Church. Below this spirit are the following:

- Main guide—a spirit who represents the Jefe del Cuadro
- Protective guides—spirits who are responsible for protecting the medium
- Spiritual guides—spirits who help the medium to guide others or to perform the "work," i.e., healing, counseling, and so forth

8

"GOD, MY SAINTS, AND MICHAELA TOO!"

Patrick Arthur Polk

Padre nuestro que estás en los cielos,
santificado sea tu nombre,
venga tu reyno,
hágase tu voluntad,
así en la tierra como en el cielo.
Danos hoy nuestro pan cotidiano,
Y perdónanos nuestras deudas,
así como nosotros perdonamos a nuestros deudores.
Y no nos metas en tentación,
mas líbranos de mal.
Amén

As always, the Friday evening mass (*misa*) at Botánica Orula in Lynwood—a small city bordering the Watts neighborhood of Los Angeles—begins with the Padre Nuestro, the Lord's Prayer. A dozen or so individuals, most clad in white, have gathered in the small chamber where the shop's proprietor, Sonia Gastelum, keeps her spiritual altar (*bóveda*). Seated closely together, they intone the prayer in Spanish and then listen attentively as Mercedes, one of Sonia's religious god-children, reads from Allan Kardec's *New Devotionary Spiritist Collection of Selected Prayers*. At the end of every second selec-tion, the congregants recite the Lord's Prayer and make the sign of the Holy Cross with practiced movements of their hands. When the last passage is read, Mercedes closes the slim paperback, the

8.1
Christ, candles, and clear water. Detail of Sonia Gastelum's Spiritist altar (*bóveda*). Photograph by Patrick A. Polk, Botánica Orula, Lynwood, 2004

8.2
Sonia Gastelum's *bóveda*
used at her Botánica Orula.
Photograph by Patrick A. Polk,
Botaníca Orula, Lynwood, 2004.

cover of which bears a striking image of Christ in his passion. Once more the Padre Nuestro is spoken in unison.

Sonia directs those present to cleanse themselves with holy water taken from a plastic container at the base of the altar and then begins singing a hymn with the imploring refrain "Save us, protect us." One by one, the attendees rise from their chairs, step forward, and dip their hands into the mixture of water, cologne, and flower petals. The sweet-smelling liquid is rubbed over heads, shoulders, arms, and upper legs in a ritualized sequence. A snap of the wrist disperses any spirit-draining impurities deposited by the trials and tribulations of daily life. The assembled quickly and lightly tap their fingertips on the table (*mesa*) that serves as the foundation for the altar before returning to their seats.

The *misa* is now "open," meaning that all are purified, "concentrated," and ready to communicate with the spirit world. Sonia instructs them to focus their attention on the altar and to open themselves to the ethereal beings who generally go unnoticed by the living except for occasions such as this. Like most *bóvedas* used by *espiritistas*, Sonia's consists of a table covered with a white cloth on which two candles, two flower vases, a statue of a Merlin-like wizard, a doll depicting a nun, and a number of clear vessels—a medium-sized glass bowl and nine tall drinking glasses—containing fresh, clean water have been carefully arranged (fig. 8.2). A miniature crucifix is affixed to the wall directly above the altar. A little higher are three mass-produced depictions of Christ, a chromolithograph of the Virgen Caridad del Cobre, the patron saint of Cuba, and a plaque showing Mary as the Virgen de Guadalupe. The wall to the left of the *bóveda* is adorned with representations of Native Americans.

The overhead light has been turned off, accentuating the flickering glow of the candles. Sonia instructs the members of the group to share any visions or psychic impressions that come to them during the ceremony. After a moment of silence, she is the first to utter the phrase "Con el permiso de la mesa" (With the permission of the table), signaling the receipt of a spiritual message. She asks a man seated across from her if he has pains in his back, describing the symptoms in detail. He nods his head in agreement, and Sonia offers a remedy. This interchange is followed by another hushed period of contemplation. Soon she again utters "With the permission of the table" and addresses a quandary faced by another individual. For more than an hour, those present in the room peer expectantly at the water-filled glasses and bowl searching for signs in the reflected candlelight and listening to the generally cryptic visions occasionally

8.3
Facade of Botánica Orula.
Photograph by Patrick A. Polk,
Lynwood, 2003.

8.4
Seasonal Halloween decoration
playfully modified to serve as
signage for Botánica Orula.
Photograph by Patrick A. Polk,
Lynwood, 2004.

related by fellow congregants. Sonia and her daughter Charlene, however, speak most often, primarily offering straightforward but crucial bits of advice.

After most of the attendees have received at least one message directed specifically to them, Sonia signals Mercedes to read more selections from the book of prayers. The Padre Nuestro and a second spiritual cleansing follow. This time the lyrics of the accompanying song announce the departure of the ceremony's invisible guests: "Se van los seres" (The beings are leaving). When the last of the embodied participants has finished the ritual bath, the container of holy water is carried out the front door and poured onto the street. It's late in the evening and the *misa* is now closed as is the botánica.

The commercial district surrounding Botánica Orula is an active urban environment: heavy traffic moves back and forth during rush hour; shoppers enter and exit stores; children walk to and from school; hungry customers line up at the take-out windows of taco stands and burger joints. Unfortunately, it is also an area where you learn to avoid eye contact. Like the concentrated gazes employed during the *misa*, averted ones are magical too. But in this case, they offer ready and perhaps protective responses to the social problems that plague this and similar neighborhoods—making them momentarily invisible.

Botánica Orula's recessed doorway and undersized sign are easy to miss (fig. 8.3). Sonia, an *espiritista* and *santera* who has operated this and other botánicas for many years, clearly doesn't depend on eye-catching signage to bring in clients. Although people do drive significant distances to see her, one gets the sense that many, if not most, of her customers walk to the shop. She describes the botánica as a neighborhood resource, one she runs with assistance from several of her children, most notably her son Shawn who is a *babalawo*, or diviner.

Mainly clients seek help with health-related problems, legal issues, and family disturbances. Sonia prefers not to get involved with affairs of the heart, and she is also adamant about not engaging in ill-intended practices (*brujería*). "Yes, we've got black candles," she remarks, "because people come in, they've got their own thing going, and it's a business. I've got to pay my rent.... But don't ask me nothing about black magic, cause I would not tell you even if I knew."

Regarding the emotional needs and pressing concerns of clients, Sonia repeatedly suggests that she should probably have taken psychology courses in her younger days. This is more a commentary on the nature of the issues she routinely encounters in her work than a critique of her own skills.

> Sometimes I really have to think to try to help that person. Cause there's been women that come in here, they're in the bottom of the pit, they want to kill their husbands. They're thinking about how to kill them because they're jealous that they're fooling around.... I go, "You don't go that way." I gotta sit them down even if it takes me two or three hours to try to get some sense into their head and to see the light, to take life differently.

Concerning the troubled youths and prostitutes who now frequently come in off the street seeking help, she notes, "They ask me, 'What can I do?' I tell them what's happening.... I show them we're into God.... Sometimes we have to have a belief in something to get out."

8.5
Sonia Gastelum seated next to her *bóveda*. Photograph by Patrick A. Polk, Botánica Orula, Lynwood, 2004.

Born in El Salvador and brought to Los Angeles by her parents when she was a year old, Sonia thinks she has probably always had psychic abilities but didn't realize the nature of her gift until she was in her late teens. The premonitions or spiritual messages that come into her mind initially disconcerted her. She recalls, "I didn't know what it was, and that's why I thank God I didn't get in a lot of trouble." Soon though, she began to harness her talent for recognizing the sources of other peoples' illnesses and personal dilemmas and furnishing appropriate remedies. In spite of her increasing work as a medium, Sonia relates that she herself was still involved in things she shouldn't have been—she whispers the words "gangs and stuff"—and needed additional positive direction to her life. Accordingly, on October 19, 1990, she was initiated as a *santera* with Obatalá as her main *oricha*. Of this divinity's influence, she asserts, "It calmed me down. It changed my life."

Like other *espiritistas*, Sonia believes that she is assisted in her work by several otherworldly beings, deceased humans whom death has transformed into heavenly helpers. Conceptualized as friends, confidants, and wardens, they often

8.6
Figures of Saint Lazarus (left), the Gypsy Irak (center), and the Native American spirit guide of Sonia's granddaughter Hadé (right). Photograph by Don Cole, Lynwood, 2004.

8.7
Sonia's consultation room featuring an altar with images of her spiritual helpers including a painting of the Gypsy Irak, a nun, several Africans, angels, Native Americans, and the Buddha. Photograph by Don Cole, Lynwood, 2004.

appear to her in dreams, and she routinely feels their presence around her, affecting her personality, shaping her character, and directing her behavior. There is a protective Native American spirit, whose name she won't divulge, who warns her of approaching dangers and guards the botánica. An ethereal Gypsy woman (*gitana*) named Irak directs her when she reads the tarot cards for clients (fig. 8.6). When Irak is "around her," Sonia relates, "I feel different. I feel more sexy, like I want to be wearing blouses and going out to dance and things.... I feel younger." Concerning this aspect of the Gypsy's presence, Sonia laughingly declares, "She's the one that gets me in trouble."

Sonia's primary guide is a female African spirit named Michaela. "She's been with me for as long as I can remember," she declares. It was this spirit being, in fact, who inspired her to open a botánica in the first place. Sonia had been practicing out of her home, but Michaela directed her to establish a botánica so she could help more people. She communicates with Sonia through visions or by speaking to her, not so much in a voice but via thoughts that flash through her head. She tells her what she can and cannot do for clients, what is the best way

8.8
Doll (upper center) used to represent Michaela, Sonia's primary spirit guide. The smaller doll (right) is one of many spiritual children of Michaela, which Sonia gives to her religious godchildren. Photograph by Patrick A. Polk, Botánica Orula, Lynwood, 2004.

of solving issues, and hints at events that are going to transpire. Occasionally during *misas*, Sonia directly channels Michaela. "She comes and tells people what's going to happen. She doesn't talk about herself, but she talks a lot about God...to believe in what's going on right now." Michaela doesn't manifest that way often, however, just when people are in dire need of help.

Sonia keeps an ornately dressed Black doll stationed on top of a display case near the front of her botánica (fig. 8.8). This is a material representation of Michaela at which clients routinely leave offerings—flowers, perfume, and little bottles of liquor—as gifts, sometimes maintaining they saw her in a dream. Although the doll is childlike in appearance, Sonia describes the spirit it symbolizes as an elderly slave woman who lived in the countryside perhaps on a plantation. "She would help people cure themselves of sickness. She died old, old." According to Sonia, although Michaela had no children, she did have many people who loved her because of the assistance she gave them. Michaela could get mad sometimes, when people didn't follow her advice. "She would say bad words. She'll be strict in that way: 'You have to listen to me.'"

Sonia states that Michaela has helped her in other important ways: "As the years have gone by she's the one who has been teaching me about sewing.... there was one point that I wanted to get away from the other kind of life that I was in and I said 'Lord, guide me so I can go on a good path and take me away from all my bad friends.'" In addition to running her botánica, Sonia started fashioning ritual garments for fellow practitioners of Santería, an activity she greatly enjoys.

When I ask her about other messages she has received from her spirit guides, Sonia responds, "When my brother [Lloyd] was going to get shot, you can even ask him, Michaela came to me." Lloyd was getting ready to go out for the evening, and Sonia warned him, "Don't go out today. Stay here. Something could happen to you." She could hear Michaela's voice saying "Tell him not to go." At about nine forty-five that night, when a friend of Lloyd's rushed into Sonia's home, she didn't need to be told that her sibling had been the victim of a drive-by shooting.

Following an eight-hour operation, during which he had a heart attack, Lloyd fell into a coma that lasted almost a month. Sonia would come and sit by him and pray to God and her spirits to help him. One day she sneaked a pigeon into his room and performed a cleansing rite by passing the bird over his body to purify him. She also kissed his face and put some Holy Water in his mouth.

Two days later Lloyd came out of the coma. Summing up her actions and the apparent result, Sonia declares, "These are things that people don't understand, and it does happen. When it does happen, they know there is another life, and there are spirits."

—————— ⋄•⋄ ——————

"When were you here last?" Sonia asks shortly after I enter the botánica. "Saturday," I reply. "We got bad news on Sunday," she says quietly. Continuing in a subdued tone she informs me that Martin Lozoya, her godchild in Santería and one of her son Shawn's best friends, had been killed in a drive-by shooting. "He was seventeen years old. They shot him three times." It happened in Baldwin Park at about ten o'clock Sunday evening. He died on the way to the hospital. His last words were "Tell my mom I love her." The police declared the incident gang related, but Sonia maintains that Martin wasn't in a gang. "He was into our spiritual things and our *collares* [beaded necklaces] and stuff." She continues, "He was gonna graduate. His grades went up. And everything. For all of us it's been a shock."

In the days leading up to the shooting, Sonia had premonitions that something terrible was going to happen. She dreamt of shoes—lots of shoes— but could not see the feet. She told her daughters that somebody was going to die, not a member of the immediate family, but a person close to them. The day before Martin was killed, she also felt a presence in her home as if someone came in and then left. Sonia didn't know who or what it was at the time but now feels that it foretold the tragic event. "That's what Espiritismo is," she asserts, "You can feel it sometimes. You can feel something coming, but God hasn't given us that gift to say 'That is the one.' He leaves mysteries inside of us. But we knew that something was coming."

Martin's mother, Mona, asked Sonia what should be done with his beads. According to tradition they would have to be destroyed. "There's a ceremony we have to do," explains Sonia. "Oh that's sad. I've been to two of those. That's a sad ceremony." It's especially heartrending in this case because of Martin's young age and the fact that he was an only child. Tragic as it seems, it is nonetheless an everyday reality in this community. Concerning this fact, Sonia states, "That's why we have the saying that 'God just lends us our kids.' He just lends them to us. We don't know when they're going to go." The senselessness of the killing, however, causes her to add, "But not that way. Not for no reason. Not for no reason."

—————— ⋄•⋄ ——————

The large playpen situated behind the botánica's front desk belongs to Sonia's granddaughter Hadé. She often babysits the child at the shop, and clients who come to visit Sonia are accustomed to encountering the toddler as well. When Hadé was born, Michaela gave Sonia a vision of the child's spiritual protector. "I saw this light coming down from the ceiling actually, and I saw the spirit that's her main guide." The proud grandmother states that the entity is an Indian princess and for this reason she has placed a Native American doll next to the

8.9
Statue of La Virgen Caridad
del Cobre, patroness of Cuba
and Catholic counterpart of the
oricha Ochún. Photograph by
Don Cole, Botánica Orula,
Lynwood, 2004.

8.10
Throne (*trono*) for Ochún, the *oricha* of Sonia's granddaughter Hadé, erected at Sonia's home. Photograph by Patrick A. Polk, Lynwood, 2003.

8.11
Detail of the *trono* for Ochún featuring beaded necklace (*collares de mazo*), metal ornamental crown, and the decorated Chinese soup tureen (*sopera*) in which Ochún's sacred stones (*otánes*) and other ritual items are secreted. Photograph by Patrick A. Polk, Lynwood, 2003.

large statue of the Virgen Caridad del Cobre stationed at the front of the shop (fig. 8.9). "I'm going to have to show my granddaughter what it is as she's growing up," Sonia says. Caridad looks after the child as well. Although only fifteen months old, Hadé has already been initiated into Santería as a priestess of Ochún.

Certain that Hadé is spiritually gifted, Sonia testifies that the child does things others her age or older would not do, such as showing clients the exact products they are looking for or don't yet know they need. Once Sonia opened the botánica in a hurry and forgot to purify herself. Hadé pointed to the Holy Water, reminding her of her obligation. "Sometimes we even look at her and we get surprised," Sonia declares. "She's something else." Epiphanies do not come solely at the price of adult pain and suffering, they can be discerned in the actions of children as well. Perhaps this is why images of the crucified Christ are so often balanced with beatific depictions of the Holy Child. Framed by knowledge of loss and sacrifice, the saving grace of Heaven, manifested in spirit-filled youth, is that much more evident. ✦

HERMANO CARLOS
AND SAN SIMÓN

Patrick Arthur Polk and Michael Owen Jones

What I believe is all about San Simón. God first, and then San Simón. Yes, I believe. Because without God and San Simón, I would not be what I am.

HERMANO CARLOS

O powerful San Simón, I, a humble being discarded by everyone, come to prostrate myself before you so that your spirit may help me in all my deeds and in every danger I have to confront. If it is a matter of love, you will get me the one I want; if it is about business matters, let them never fail because your spirit will not allow evil ones to have more power than you; if it concerns hidden enemies, it is you who has to make them go (away) as soon as I call your name.

EXCERPT FROM A POPULAR PRAYER TO SAN SIMÓN

"My name is Carlos Arana Figueroa Martínez. I'm from Guatemala. I was born on November 8th, 1959. I'm from a village called Samayac Suchitepéquez. I come from a family of many; I have an uncle whose name is Perú and another one whose name is Francisco García. They are witches [*brujos*] since birth and I am too" (fig. 9.2).[1] It is strange to hear Martínez, known to us informally as "Hermano Carlos," describe himself as a *brujo*, although the image conjured up by the term might seem to receive support from the two golden stars inlayed in his front teeth and his fantastically ornamented consultation room. Carlos advertises using the sobriquet

9.1
Statue of San Simón with offerings and decorations in Botánica y Templo San Simón de los Llanos. Photograph by Don Cole, Los Angeles, 2004.

9.2
Hermano Carlos with a statue of San Simón held in his right hand and a statue of a spirit, or *duende*, associated with magic and wealth in his left hand. Photograph by Patrick A. Polk, Botánica y Templo San Simón de los Llanos, Los Angeles, 2000.

9.3
Hermano Carlos's consultation room festooned with Guatemalan masks, a portrait of himself in a feathered headdress, and a variety of religious icons. Photograph by Don Cole, Botánica y Templo San Simón de los Llanos, Los Angeles, 2004.

"The *curandero* from Samayac," and we've followed his practice as a healer and spiritual advisor for some time. It is difficult to reconcile ingrained perceptions of "witches" with our observations of a *curandero* who works primarily with the Guatemalan folk saint San Simón.[2] Asked to clarify his choice of words, Carlos responds, "I said *witch* because that's how people call me. In the place where I come from they say there is a good man who can cure you." Addressing the source of our puzzlement, he continues, "Here, people use *witch* to insult a person." He's right. Some folk concepts just don't translate well in El Norte. Nonetheless, they're still crucial to one's sense of self. And so, Hermano Carlos, the *curandero* and *espiritista*, remains above all a *brujo*. It is as much a part of his identity as are his name, birth date, and birthplace, even if it does cause some to see him in a more culturally negative light or, worse, to come to him with evil purposes in mind.

By the age of eight Carlos knew he had special powers, but he did not start working with spirits until after he was married, and then not by choice. He remembers: "I would be talking when all of a sudden I would just fall. My wife would get scared and run out the room, she would leave me there and go call my Aunt Virgilia, and she is a bit of a Spiritist and she would come and she would talk and she would give counsel." Guided by Virgilia, Carlos developed his abilities and now works with a number of spirits, most of whom he identifies as deceased family members and noted healers who lived in Guatemala. Among them are uncles and aunts—Brother Rodolfo, Brother Ronaldo, Brother Francisco García, Brother Fidelino Figueroa, and Sister Catalina—as well as his mother, Rosa Figueroa, and his grandmother, Francisca Orizaba. "It's with them that I work. If I ask them to cure someone, I can cure them."

9.4
Flanked by angels, San Simón stands guard over the entrance to a small sanctuary. Photograph by Patrick A. Polk, Botánica y Templo San Simón de los Llanos, Los Angeles, 2000.

Hermano Carlos became aware of San Simón as a child when he began working at a *barrotería*, or a store selling food and liquor. The owner believed in the saint so Carlos helped build an altar in the store, and every Tuesday and Friday the two of them would put an image of San Simón outside to attract customers. Describing the saint's origin, Carlos recounts his version of a well-known legend that tells how a European medical practitioner was transformed into a Guatemalan folk saint.

> He came from Italy and when he arrived, he chose a place where the poor lived and this place was called Zunil.... He became very famous because he would give out medicine, money, vaccines, and he would protect people.... And everyone liked him, but those people who envied him wanted to kill him. They would say that he was not a doctor but a witch.... They didn't let him work and prohibited him to give anything to people.... Since they wanted to kill him, the Indians would protect him.

With the help of some Maya, the Italian doctor traveled toward Guatemala City in order to escape his persecutors. While on his journey he stopped at an isolated house on a mountain path in the place that would later become San Andrés Itzapa. There a mysterious old man greeted him and offered him coffee. After drinking from the cup, the Italian was transformed into San Simón. "Now," claims Carlos, "this saint is very miraculous in Guatemala. Whatever you ask him, he will grant it."

9.6
San Simón from Chichicaste-
nango, Guatemala. Collection
of Jim Pieper. Photograph by
Don Cole, Los Angeles, 2004.

9.7
Guatemalan San Simón
effigies. Collection of Jim
Pieper. Photograph by Don
Cole, Los Angeles, 2004.

9.5 (opposite)
San Simón altar from
Olintepeque, Quetzaltenango,
Guatemala. Collection of Jim
Pieper. Photograph by Don
Cole, Los Angeles, 2004.

9.8
San Simón from Yepocapa,
Chimaltenango, Guatemala.
Collection of Jim Pieper.
Photograph by Don Cole,
Los Angeles, 2004.

9.9
Exterior of Botánica y Templo
San Simón de los Llanos.
Photograph by Patrick A. Polk,
Los Angeles, 2000.

Following a migration fraught with life-threatening situations, Carlos arrived in Los Angeles on February 25, 1988. He ascribes the ultimate success of his difficult journey to the divine intercession of God and San Simón. He initially worked at a number of jobs including cleaning houses, construction, and tree trimming before opening Botánica San Simón de los Llanos in 1994 (fig. 9.9). Hermano Carlos treats a wide variety of ailments, provides *limpias* (spiritual cleansings), and performs *trabajos*, or "works" (the removing or casting of spells). Citing the ethnic backgrounds of his clientele, he lists Belizeans, Guatemalans, Arabs, Iranians, Chinese, Filipinos, Jamaicans, Hondurans, Salvadorans, and Nicaraguans—also Europeans and Anglo-Americans, but in much fewer numbers. He is proud of his trade and would very much like to be accepted, if not utilized, by the mainstream medical care profession. "If I was given an opportunity to work in a hospital," he says, "I could do it.... Here, it is too bad that they do not allow one to grow. If you do not have a degree from a university, you are not taken seriously." Asked if he would aid a medical doctor if requested to do so, he replies, "Yes, but that's never going to happen [laughs] so what's the use in talking about that."

The majority of his clients, Carlos maintains, come seeking assistance with health issues, troublesome personal relationships, economic dilemmas, and immigration status. More specifically, he is sought out by alcoholics and sufferers of all sorts of physical ailments; women who have been mistreated or emotionally abused by spouses or lovers; undocumented workers who have been exploited by employers or coworkers and feel they have nowhere else to turn; unemployed laborers who hope that San Simón can open up a position for them; and migrants whose permanent resident status is in question or who have had to cross the border any way they could. Concerning this last need, Carlos recounted for us the case of a woman who had come to him for help with the INS:

> They asked her for a current passport, she needed some paperwork adjustments done. They asked her for an I.D. but she didn't have an I.D. She didn't have an I.D. or an interpreter with her. In fact, she didn't have an appointment that day, and she was able to get in. Generally, you have to have an appointment with immigration or you don't get in. But, she got in. You see, she had been praying to San Simón. The agent told her that because she was an honest woman he was going to help her. The agent was very nice to her. He filled out a passport form for her because she didn't have one, signed her paperwork, and she was done. Lots of people come here to see San Simón because he performs a lot of miracles.

As Carlos understands all too well from his own experiences, many immigrants face serious hurdles in the quest to earn a decent living in Los Angeles due to lack of English-language proficiency and education or specialized training, as well as the overarching problem of their legal immigration status. He explains, "These people have a lot of faith in God, San Simón, and me, and they come to me."

"HE COMES TO ME IN DREAMS"

While San Simón communicates with some individuals through meditation or mediumship, he comes to Carlos in dreams. In one of them, Carlos found himself on a grassy hill far away. It was surrounded by barbed wire, and at first, San Simón appeared to be wearing a uniform similar to that worn by the U.S. Border Patrol. Soon, however, Carlos saw the more recognizable short blue pants, small worn-out jacket, and rubber boots. The saint looked to be about thirty years old, had dark brown skin like a Native American, and was growing a mustache. Addressing Carlos, he said, "I'm Simón and I want to talk to you." San Simón then proceeded to diagnose the illness that was troubling one of Carlos's patients and informed him that she would be cured. Carlos notes, "He tells me what is going to happen. He always tells me things in dreams but I don't always remember."

San Simón may appear to clients as well. Asked about extraordinary cures, Hermano Carlos told of an experience with a severely ill child who was brought to him from Guatemala. The child's parents had sneaked him out of a hospital in Guatemala because they felt he wasn't receiving proper treatment. The parents were *coyotes* (smugglers of immigrants) so they were able to get the boy to Los Angeles quickly. The mother was caught and sent back, but the father made it into the country and brought the dying child—hospital IV needle and tubing still dangling from his arm—to Hermano Carlos for treatment. Through the help of God and San Simón, Carlos reported that he was able to effect a cure. Afterward the child was taken to a hospital to have the IV apparatus removed from his arm as the needle was deeply imbedded. While at the hospital, some members of an evangelical church came to pray for the boy. The child, however, told them not

9.10
San Simón shrine. Photograph
by Don Cole, Botánica y Templo
San Simón de los Llanos, Los
Angeles, 2004.

to because "the man with the hat cured me." One of the evangelicals asked if he was referring to the popular Mexican singer Vicente Fernández. "No," the child replied, "it was a man named Simón. He cured me and he wears a hat!" "You're talking about a singer," the evangelical argued. "No," the boy responded, "He's over at a church and he's a saint from Guatemala and he cured me and he's right here with me." The child could see San Simón at his side. "Here he is and he cured me." With regard to such purported miracles and the importance of San Simón in his life, Carlos exclaimed, "He is my everything!"

In keeping with his devotion and spiritual practice, Carlos has allocated half of the space in his botánica to a *templo* (temple) for San Simón. Approximately twelve feet wide by thirty feet long, the temple contains at one end an altar featuring a nearly life-size representation of a seated San Simón enshrined in an open-fronted glass case (fig. 9.10). Satin cloth serves as a backdrop, draped behind the straight-backed chair that serves as his throne. Fresh flowers in vases stand on either side. A large bouquet rests on the saint's lap. The encased figure is elevated on a raised platform flanked by smaller statues of San Simón—along with the Virgin Mary, Jesus Christ, and other holy personages—as well as offerings of food, drink, and cigarettes. A table in front of the shrine holds dozens of lighted glass candles, or *velas*. Supplicants have placed more burning candles on the floor under and around the table and three fire extinguishers hang on the walls. In a corner at the opposite end of the room stand crutches left by individuals who have miraculously regained the functioning of their limbs. The air is heavy with fragrance, the temperature ten to fifteen degrees hotter than outside.

San Simón's physical appearance and accoutrements can differ significantly from shrine to shrine in Guatemala and the United States. He is often dressed to resemble authoritarian figures—presidents, generals, mayors, judges, policemen, and so on—complete with uniform, rod or staff of office, and official insignia. Other commonplace guises include that of a dapper man wearing a fashionable black suit and hat and that of a laborer dressed in a straw hat, dark shirt and pants, and heavy shoes. "Whatever you can put on him," says Carlos. "I've had San Simón with indigenous [*indígena*] clothing. In Guatemala they have him dressed as a lieutenant, president, or mayor." On several occasions Hermano Carlos has told us that his altar and San Simón replicate those of San Andrés Itzapa, a popular shrine located at the place where Simón was transformed into a saint. As is the case at that shrine, San Simón is depicted as a light-complexioned and mustachioed adult wearing a cowboy hat, a black suit, white dress shirt, a dark necktie, and polished cowboy boots. Seated in a chair, he holds a wooden rod in his right hand and a brightly colored towel or a strip of Guatemalan textile is draped over his lap. Sometimes a cigarette or cigar is placed in his mouth or one of his hands.

Hermano Carlos maintains that his temple and, more specifically, the large effigy of San Simón are community resources. Individuals bring bouquets of flowers to place in the lap of the saint, and they even dress him. Cigarettes are lit, puffed on twice, and then placed in the mouth of one or another of the smaller

9.11
Statue at the chapel (*capilla*) of San Simón in San Andrés Itzapa, Chimaltenango, Guatemala. Photograph by Jim Pieper.

9.12
Shrine room for San Simón in San Andrés Itzapa, Chimaltenango, Guatemala. This site served as the model for the temple established in Los Angeles by Hermano Carlos. Photograph by Jim Pieper.

9.13
Detail of shrine with miniature San Simón figures and offerings at the Botánica y Templo San Simón de los Llanos. Photograph by Don Cole, Los Angeles, 2004.

9.14
Portable platform (*casita*) used to carry a statue of San Simón during the annual fiesta for the saint held in late October. Photograph by Don Cole, Botánica y Templo San Simón de los Llanos, Los Angeles, 2004.

replicas flanking the large statue (fig. 9.13). Some people bring liquor, take a shot, and leave the rest for the saint. They ask for his help and offer the toast "¡Qué viva San Simón!" (Long live San Simón!). Believers often whisper their requests in his right ear, a mode of pleading that is thought to be especially efficacious because "you are talking to him directly." Some write letters that they place in the hand of the large figure, or they bring photographs of those who have mistreated them, petitioning San Simón for protection or retribution. They put the photos under San Simón's left foot, said to be the one that he uses to dominate. Carlos relates, "People write a letter saying that they need their husbands; they need work, that their husband doesn't leave them. It's mostly for work. So that the Americans won't treat them badly. Things like that."

¡QUÉ VIVA SAN SIMÓN!

In association with the local Brotherhood of San Simón (Cofradía de San Simón), a lay association to which he belongs, Hermano Carlos plays host to an annual festival held on a Sunday in late October, on or near the feast day of San Simón (October 28). Mostly attended by Central Americans, the festivities include a procession during which worshipers place a statue of San Simón on a portable

9.15
Hermano Carlos and fellow worshiper bearing San Simón's *casita* through the streets near Botánica y Templo San Simón de los Llanos. Photograph by Patrick A. Polk, Los Angeles, 2002.

9.16
During the San Simón procession, originating at Botánica y Templo San Simón de los Llanos, male and female congregants take turns carrying the saint. Photograph by Patrick A. Polk, Los Angeles, 2000.

platform (*casita*) and "walk" the saint through the streets near the botánica-temple (figs. 9.14–9.16). Participants take turns hoisting the *casita* bearing the saint onto their shoulders while swinging back and forth to the music of a marching band. The parade ends at a tented parking lot behind the botánica where the congregants welcome San Simón with his favorite song "El Rey de Mil Coronas" (The King of a Thousand Crowns). Later, people perform traditional dances; a group of women in native costume enact a story through dance of how one of them was healed with herbs; and food, beer, and soft drinks abound. Throughout the event many visit the temple, light candles, and pray to San Simón.

At the festival for San Simón held on October 22, 2000, several people who entered the temple talked about what the saint had done for them. One woman from Guatemala said, "For me, San Simón is the best. He is great and he has given me all I've asked him for. He is lovely, he is powerful, and that's why I *love* San Simón. *¡Qué viva San Simón!*" She went on to say, "Four years ago I started believing in San Simón. I didn't believe in him before, but now I love him, and *¡qué viva San Simón!*" When asked what miracles the saint had performed for her, she related, "I'm not living with my husband now. He took my two girls with him to Mexico, and I asked San Simón to bring them back to me, and he did.

9.17
Participants at the San Simón
fiesta organized by the Cofradía
de San Simón, a lay religious
organization with which Hermano
Carlos is associated, pose for the
camera. Photograph by Patrick
A. Polk, Los Angeles, 2003.

That's why I love San Simón." She said that she visits
the saint at this temple "when I need him to help
me with something, and I bring him some flowers."
An active devotee, well-known to Hermano Carlos,
she was allowed the honor of dressing the temple's
main statue of San Simón on this day. She replaced
his shoes with a pair of light blue ostrich-skin boots
that she had brought as a votive offering. "They're
not very expensive, but for me they don't cost anything if they are for someone as wonderful as he is,
and he's worthy of something even more expensive."

Another woman who had also emigrated from
Guatemala said, "The first time I heard about San
Simón was when a friend of mine who's very devoted
to him told me that he had done many miracles,
so that's when I started believing in him." On this
feast day she brought flowers for the altar. Asked
why she was devoted to him, she replied, "The first
great thing he did for me was to help me pass the
citizenship test when I didn't know how to speak a
bit of English. There was also another time when
I crossed the border through Tijuana with two kids
[her niece and nephew]. They didn't do anything
to me. They just arrested me and took one of the
kids with them, and I had prayed to him so much that nothing really happened.
I could have lost my green card."

Attendance at the festival, in and of itself, is thought to bestow blessings,
health, and good fortune on participants and bystanders. Carlos told us of a young
woman who was suffering from stomach cancer who "couldn't dance, her bones
hurt, she couldn't eat because as soon as she ate something she would throw it
back up." Her husband parked their car near where the procession would pass.
When the celebrants arrived, smoke from the burning incense wafted inside the
car. The husband told the young woman to close all the windows and to have
faith in the smoke because it would heal her. She did, and as a result, Carlos
maintains, "She felt better and she was able to eat and dance."

As we left the festival held in 2000, Hermano Carlos thanked us for coming
and asked if we had gotten any of the chicken stew, rice, and tamales being served
to guests. We said that we had and commented that they were excellent. "I'm so
happy you ate some of our food," he responded. His face was still beaming with
pleasure as he led us back to the table where several women were preparing meals
and helped them bag up extra tamales for us to take home. At this moment,
something he had said in an earlier interview suddenly made much more sense.
"I am always happy with American people that don't reject my food," Carlos
announced when we had first asked him about the importance of the festival. "I like
it when you are very open." Viewed within the context of San Simón's legend,

9.18
Hermano Carlos and San Simón.
Photograph by Patrick A. Polk,
Los Angeles, Botánica y Templo
San Simón de los Llanos, 2003.

personal narratives recounting his divine assistance, and the fiesta held in his behalf, it is this same exchange of honor and hospitality that sometimes transforms persecuted foreigners into honored guests if not saints, that rescues misunderstood healers who have been called witches for the wrong reasons, and that turns lonely mountainsides or urban storefronts into holy sites. For a *brujo* from Samayac, it's another sure sign that the barbed wire fences are behind him and that San Simón continues to open ways through barriers and borders or to tear them down entirely.

Drawing on traditions of faith and reacting to lived experience in Los Angeles, individuals turn to San Simón and folk practitioners such as Hermano Carlos when anxious and under stress and when seeking answers to problems that do not admit ready solutions, such as making ends meets, migrating to and living in an unfamiliar place, finding a soul mate, holding a family together, treating chronic illness, or protecting oneself in a dangerous environment. Often the nature of an adherent's trouble is clear-cut, whether cancer, loneliness, fear, unemployment, domestic violence, or immigration status. Sadly, though, understanding the immediate source of a problem does not mean that it is easily remedied or rectified. Thus, for those faced with seemingly insurmountable difficulties, a cause for hope can be found through the guidance of San Simón. ⟠

10 INFINITE GESTURES

Franco Mondini-Ruiz's *Infinito Botánica: L.A.*

Miki Garcia

> *It is hard to be finite upon an infinite subject, and all subjects are infinite.*
>
> HERMAN MELVILLE

For the last ten years artist Franco Mondini-Ruiz has been creating sculptures, paintings, performances, and traveling installations inspired by the mestizo culture of Mexican Americans from South Texas. Born in Boerne, Texas, to a Chicana mother and an Italian father, Mondini-Ruiz draws upon his own diverse background to investigate issues of class, race, gender, and diversity. The cultural tensions that existed between his upper middle-class European father and his working-class Tejana mother are the seeds of self-discovery that Mondini-Ruiz uses as the basis of his work.

Trained as a lawyer, Mondini-Ruiz left a successful practice in the early 1990s and purchased a botánica in a Mexican American barrio in San Antonio, Texas. Mondini-Ruiz kept the original name of the store, *Infinito Botánica and Gift Shop*, and all of its original faith-healing merchandise, consisting of candles, potions, and herbs. In addition, pre-Columbian artifacts, Spanish colonial antiques, wares from local artisans, and other miscellany could be found at his botánica. Mixed into this eclectic assemblage were also artworks for sale by contemporary Mexican and Texas artists Alejandro Diaz, Cisco Jimenez, Michael Tracy, Chuck Ramirez, Jesse Amado, Mary Jesse Garza, Anne Wallace, Elizabeth McGrath, and Mondini-Ruiz himself (Diaz 1999).

10.1
Franco Mondini-Ruiz. *Infinito Botánica: L.A.*, 2004. Mixed media. 4.88 x 10.36 x .85 m. Commissioned by the UCLA Fowler Museum of Cultural History. Photograph by Don Cole.

10.1a–d
Details of figure 10.1.

10.2
Infinito Botánica and Gift Shop, San Antonio. Mondini-Ruiz purchased this botánica located in a Mexican American barrio in the early 1990s. He retained the original merchandise, transforming it with his own eclectic mix of objects and decor. Photograph courtesy of the artist.

Mondini-Ruiz owned and operated *Infinito Botánica and Gift Shop*, re-stocking merchandise and chatting with customers about his life and art. His natural ease as a salesman may have stemmed from early childhood when the artist spent many hours behind the counter of the Mondini family's electronics store. But the compulsion to initiate *Infinito Botánica* as an artistic endeavor signaled a deeper exploration of identity and sense of place. *Infinito Botánica* was ultimately a laboratory for experimenting with aesthetics and notions of high versus low culture, exoticization and authenticity, queer theory, Mexican American identity, and so forth. Out of this process, the artist created exquisitely wrought hybrid sculpture consisting of the most incongruous elements: fruit pies with porcelain figures affixed to them or plaster statues dancing arm in arm with pre-Columbian fertility goddesses. By consciously integrating seemingly disparate objects and ideas, Mondini-Ruiz was able to celebrate what was not considered beautiful by mainstream standards.

Infinito Botánica transformed a local shop into an art gallery, salon, and ongoing performance piece. Mondini-Ruiz created a world of his own where hybrid and absurd ideas could be brought together to reflect a more nuanced and representative reality (*mondini* incidentally is Italian for "little worlds"). The botánica quickly became a destination for the cultural elite from San Antonio and beyond; poems were written about it, art was inspired by it, and for a time, it became a cultural center, adopting those who did not seem to "fit" anywhere else. Of this time, Mondini-Ruiz has said, "The important thing is that the Botánica became a haven for those who felt fragmented: it became a metaphor for a more accurate picture of identity and attracted people from every race, class, ethnicity and religion"(personal communication, 2004).

INFINITO BOTÁNICA INSTALLATIONS ON TOUR

Mondini-Ruiz closed *Infinito Botánica and Gift Shop* in 1999 but nevertheless continues to present versions of it in galleries and museums throughout the world, further exploring the nature of performance, commercial enterprise, and globalization. Re-situated in the formal space of the "white cube," Mondini-Ruiz acquires and presents objects ranging from discarded jewel cases, perfume bottles, and items culled from local markets to high-end bric-a-brac from familiar retail stores arranged within the framework of the modernist grid. The first incarnation of *Infinito Botánica* to take place outside the actual shop occurred in 1996, following a residency at ArtPace, San Antonio. Palm fronds and other flora, religious icons, seventeenth-century porcelains, and gleaming objets d'art sat atop white pedestals or were delicately arranged on the floor. For the artist, the introduction of his store into the space of an art gallery became a place "where a Prada boutique

10.3
Franco Mondini-Ruiz.
Gorgeous Politics, part of the
Infinito Botánica: New York
installation, 1999. Mixed media.
12 x 9 x .5 m. Photograph by
Scott Lifshutz, Bard College,
Annandale-on-Hudson, New York.

meets the barrio's botánica" (Armstrong and Zamudio-Taylor 1999, 72). As it had been in the original *Infinito Botánica and Gift Shop*, each cluster of objects or vignette adhered to the idea of *rasquachismo*, a term coined by the art historian Tomas Ybarra-Frausto to describe Chicano art as "making do" with what is available (1991). Expanding beyond the concept of resourcefulness, Mondini-Ruiz's *Infinito Botánicas* revealed a sincere attempt at beautification, reflecting the human need to personalize and adorn our most intimate spaces.

In 1999 Mondini-Ruiz participated in an exhibition at Bard College, Annandale-on-Hudson, where he produced a site-specific installation entitled *High Yellow*. The yellow and white items—Little Debbie cakes, clear crystal punch bowls, feathers, porcelain statuettes, and other tchotchkes—were assembled onto large white pedestals, each object referred to the politics of race and notions of "passing for white." Mondini-Ruiz subsequently participated in the *2000 Whitney Biennial* exhibition at the Whitney Museum of American Art in New York. The artist's two-part exhibition consisted of an *Infinito Botánica: New York* with a series of tiny white shelves installed on a wall, each presenting a different scene. The materials included the artist's trove of merchandise brought from San Antonio, items collected from local "99-Cent stores," trinkets from Chinatown stalls, Madison Avenue boutique bags and tags, and so on. The second portion recaptured the performative function of the original *Infinito Botánica*. On weekends throughout the run of the exhibition, the artist stationed himself on the sidewalk in front of the Whitney's Marcel Breuer–designed museum, peddling his wares and making trades with passersby.

Also in 1999, Mondini-Ruiz participated in a group exhibition entitled *UltraBaroque: Aspects of Post-Latin American Art* organized by the Museum of Contemporary Art, San Diego. For this traveling exhibition, the artist was invited

10.4
Franco Mondini-Ruiz.
Infinito Botánica: San Diego,
2000. Mixed media with
papier-mâché. 7 x 11 x 1 m.
Commissioned by Museum
of Contemporary Art San Diego.
Installation view at Museum of
Contemporary Art San Diego.
Photograph by Pablo Mason.

to visit the Tijuana/San Diego area for several weeks to create a site-specific installation that reflected the heterogeneous nature of the border region in California. Utilizing his trademark technique of assemblage and collecting, Mondini-Ruiz created a floor-based installation using objects in green and pink hues meant to reflect the area's tropical environment. Subsequently, each museum hosting *UltraBaroque* commissioned Mondini-Ruiz to create an installation based on the city's local culture, launching a tour of *Infinito Botánicas* around the country.[1] Each installation incorporated with it items from the place before, which were mixed with recently collected objects particular to each location.

By traveling outside its local cultural environment the *Infinito Botánica* series transcended the notion that it was important to one specific community. It thus delivered a universal message about the value of hybridity and the desire for beauty in one's life. Its eclectic form and visceral allure appealed to a diverse range of audiences outside of Texas who also sought a more inclusive depiction of contemporary art.

INFINITO BOTÁNICA: L.A.

In collaboration with the exhibition *Botánica Los Angeles: Latino Popular Religious Art in the City of Angels*, Mondini-Ruiz has created a botánica-inspired installation reflecting the contemporary cultural landscape of Los Angeles. It brings together many of the artist's past concerns: the parallelism of the botánica with contemporary desires to purify or improve, the use of humor as a form of resistance, and the notion that beauty is subjective and contextual.

Mondini-Ruiz's installation includes materials obtained from local botánicas as well as tourist shops, street vendors, and the Fowler Museum's permanent collections. *Infinito Botánica: Los Angeles* is a platform-based installation within two thousand feet of exhibition space. It addresses themes traditionally associated with Los Angeles: artifice, seduction, and desire. Whereas audiences coming to the Fowler Museum's *Botánica Los Angeles* exhibition are meant to experience the culture of spirituality and faith healing in Hispanic American societies (historical essays, authentic artifacts, and anecdotes and examples from practicing faith healers), Mondini-Ruiz uses his installation as a vehicle to investigate the culture of the botánica itself, considered as something naive, taboo, kitschy, or superstitious in a contemporary context.

Mondini-Ruiz's *Infinito Botánica: L.A.* thus acts as a bridge between Curanderismo or other Indo-Christian belief structures and contemporary U.S. life. For the artist, the botánica is a hybrid construct, an ethnic interpretation of improving your lot in life. Just as practitioners of Curanderismo seek to cure an assortment of ailments—ranging from headaches, loss of love, money problems, and aging to guilt—so too present-day Angelenos hope to achieve enlightenment through ascribing to the latest fads, buying potions and creams promising youth, and practicing the rituals of Pilates and yoga. By mixing elements of "high" and "low" culture, Mondini-Ruiz collapses these differences stating, "The rich lady buying a Donald Judd, for me, is no different than a poor lady buying a religious statue. It is humorous to me that we accepted Nancy Reagan running the country based on tarot card readings and yet someone boiling herbs for purification is somehow considered exotic" (personal communication, 2004).

CONCLUSION

Although it happened by chance, the word *infinite* is critical to understanding the trajectory of Mondini-Ruiz's oeuvre. As an acculturated light-skinned Latino, Mondini-Ruiz knew very little about his origins and culture, learning much of it from better-educated, often white southerners of South Texas. The consequent feelings of shame coupled with his unique brand of defiance compelled him to pursue a career as an artist. Through the *Infinito Botánica* series, Mondini-Ruiz engages in a process of excavation that attempts to recuperate a part of history of Mexicans (and Mexican Americans) that has been alternately wiped out or ignored. As a stranger to his own past, Mondini-Ruiz creates his own narrative, putting together fragments of what he knows and adding layers of what he desires. Every time he creates an *Infinito Botánica*, Mondini-Ruiz is creating a part of a larger story, leaving behind a unique legacy. The critical import of *Infinito Botánica* rests on its position as an infinite, multivalent, unfixed, hybrid, absorptive and ever-evolving concept. ❧

Franco Mondini-Ruiz lives and works in New York City. His work has been exhibited widely throughout the United States and has been featured in solo exhibitions in New York, Dallas, Saint Louis, San Antonio, and Mexico City. Group exhibitions include the Whitney Biennial 2000 *and* UltraBaroque: Aspects of Post-Latin American Art *(organized by the Museum of Contemporary Art, San Diego, and touring in 2000–2003 to Fort Worth, San Francisco, Miami, Toronto, and Minneapolis). He is a recipient of the 2004–2005 Rome prize.*

NOTES TO THE TEXT

CHAPTER 3 (HERNÁNDEZ AND JONES)

The research on which this essay is based was funded by Grant Number 5 R21-AT00202 from the National Center for Complementary and Alternative Medicine (NCCAM) for which Michael Owen Jones was the principal investigator. The essay's contents are solely the responsibility of the authors and do not necessarily represent the official views of NCCAM or the National Institutes of Health.

1. In the botánicas of Los Angeles, the dominant healing systems appear to be Curanderismo and Espiritismo, reflecting neighborhood demographics that indicate a Central American and Mexican majority. These shops recall the *yerberías* (herb stores) and *perfumerías* (perfumeries) found in Latin America, which sell medicinal goods, candles, incense, and other sacramental items commonly used in therapeutic rituals that are based on Amerindian customs (use of particular plants), Catholic tenets (recognition of good and evil and a supreme God), and Spiritist beliefs (affirmation of connection with ancestors as well as with spirits that can help or hinder our physical condition).

2. With the exception of Carlos Meraz, who gave permission for his name to be used in the captions to figures 3.9 and 3.10, the names of botánicas and people referred to in this essay have been changed.

CHAPTER 4 (POLK)

1. "Eshu" is the name of an avatar of Elegba (Eleguá).
2. Whereas most practitioners of Santería refer to this divinity as "Eleguá," the García Villamils use the spelling "Elegba."

CHAPTER 5 (MARTON)

1. In other words, don't get stuck in all the nonessentials and unimportant obstacles and pettiness that you might encounter. América and I conversed completely in Spanish. All translations presented in this essay are mine.

2. This approximates the saying "God helps those who help themselves."

3. I had almost entered another Santería group in Los Angeles approximately three years previously, having been told that Eleguá was saying that I should join, but I had declined. América later told me she knew and had previously, at times, oriented the other *santero* (who had given me the earlier reading) and that it was all as it should be that I had entered her house.

4. This term is nearly untranslatable. Perhaps the closest parallel would be "loving kindness."

5. Atilio, a Candomblé *pai de santo* (a spiritual leader) in Brazil, years later recounted how he, while possessed by an *oricha* (spelled *orixa* in Brazil)—other than Changó—ate *acarajé* (West African deep-fried bean cakes) dipped in boiling oil and taken directly from the hot pot as a test of the genuineness of his possession. No deleterious physiological effects—to his mouth or gastrointestinal system—resulted. Regarding possession, or "incorporation" as it is called in Brazil, I have also learned that it may involve different levels of loss of consciousness (see Marton 1986; 2002). Nevertheless deliberate faking or affectation is an entirely different matter.

CHAPTER 7 (FLORES-PEÑA)

1. Following the Cuban Revolution of 1959, Afro-Cuban religions such as Lucumí, Palo, and Cuban-style Espiritismo became widely known in Puerto Rico.

2. Spiritism and Freemasonry became the enemies of the Spanish state. The doctrines espoused by both philosophical currents were opposed to the official teachings of the Catholic Church.

3. The Arawak, or Taino, has come to embody Puerto Rico. The importance of these people is evident in Puerto Rican formal and popular arts. Individual altars to the *"indios"* grace many temples, businesses, and private homes.

4. The seal presents a Spaniard holding Nebrija'a famous Spanish-Latin dictionary of circa 1492. On one side a Taino Indian holds ears of corn and a Cemí, an Arawak icon that represents a deity. On the other side an African appears holding a cutlass and sugarcane stalks; at his feet is the Vejigante mask (a horned mask made from a coconut and painted with bright colors). This is the most respected grouping in Puerto Rican culture.

5. Although the term *Madamas* derives from the French *madame*, the word *Madamo* was coined to refer to a male spirit.

6. The iconography of these spirits resembles that of the Cuban spirits known as Africanos de nación and the Brazilian Pretos Velhos (Old Blacks).

7. These are not to be confused with the same dolls in Afro-Cuban practices. In an Afro-Cuban context they may represent a spirit who had *santo* (i.e., a spirit who had been a *santera* or a Lucumí priestess when alive or one who is aligned with these practices). The dolls may also represent a spirit associated with Palo.

8. It is essential for a medium to know the names, powers, and mission of the spirits with whom he or she is going to work. These names are secret and only the spirits themselves can reveal them. This process is not effected solely by possession;

other mediums may add information as the new medium develops.

9. Hardly performed nowadays, this spiritual marriage ceremony takes place in front of the altar. Because of the high incidence of divorce, Spiritists do not advise it. Although one can dissolve a marriage through divorce, no one can divorce the spirits.

10. I am using the Lucumí spelling, which employs the creole "ch."

11. This construct is based on where the icons are placed in relation to the earth. For example, icons placed on the floor most likely represent African spirits and ancestors. The same icon with flowers placed on high can be safely understood as representing a saint of the Church, since this is the usual setting for them. On a table with flowers and water the icon may represent a spiritual guide or protection or the saint who represents those spiritual forces.

CHAPTER 9 (POLK AND JONES)

1. This interview was conducted in Spanish with a translator present.

2. Romberg (2003) employs the term "witch-healer" as a way to address this issue.

CHAPTER 10 (GARCIA)

1. Mondini-Ruiz brought a version of *Infinito Botánica* to Fort Worth, San Francisco, Miami, Toronto, and Minneapolis.

REFERENCES CITED

Armstrong, Elizabeth, and Victor Zamudio-Taylor
1999   *Ultrabaroque: Aspects of Post-Latin American Art*. San Diego: Museum of Contemporary Art, San Diego.

Bascom, William
1969   *Ifa Divination: Communication between Gods and Men in West Africa*. Bloomington: Indiana University Press.
1980   *Sixteen Cowries: Yoruba Divination from Africa to the New World*. Bloomington: Indiana University Press.

Brown, David. H.
2003   *Santería Enthroned: Art, Ritual, and Innovation in an Afro-Cuban Religion*. Chicago: University of Chicago Press.

Carpentier, Alejo
1981   *La consagración de la primavera*. Mexico City: Siglo Veintiuno Editores.

Castro, Adrian
1997   "December 31, 1999." In *Cantos to Blood and Honey: Poems by Adrian Castro*. Minneapolis: Coffee House Press.

Chabrán, Rafael
1997   "Changing Paradigms in Chicano Studies: Ethnography, Oppositional Ethnography, and Ethnobiography." *Occasional Paper*, no. 31. East Lansing: Julian Samora Research Institute, Michigan State University.

De La Luz, Caridad
2004   "Botánicas and Fragrance Houses." <http://www.mibarrio. org/botanicas.htm>

Diaz, Alejandro
1999   "Gorgeous Politics: The Life and Work of Franco Mondini-Ruiz." M.A. thesis, Bard College.

Fernández Olmos, Margarite, and Lizabeth Paravisini-Gebert
2001   *Healing Cultures: Art and Religion as Curative Practices in the Caribbean and Its Diaspora*. New York: Palgrave.

Hufford, David
1985   "Ste. Anne de Beaupré: Roman Catholic Pilgrimage and Healing." *Western Folklore* 44, no. 3: 194–207.

Kahaner, Larry
1988   *Cults That Kill: Probing the Underworld of Occult Crime*. New York: Warner Books.

Kardec, Allan
1996   *The Spirits' Book*. Translated by Anna Blackwell. 6th ed. Brasilia: Federação Espírita Brasileira.

Kinney, Jay
1999–2001   "Five Future Religions Waiting to Happen." *Rob Breszny's Free Will Astrology*. <http://www.freewillastrology. com/beauty/beauty.main88.shtml>

Marton, Yves
1986   "The Dancing of the Orishas in Los Angeles and Pan-Yoruba Spiritual Tradition." M.A. thesis, University of California, Los Angeles.
2002   'I Saw It with My Own Eyes': An Ethnography of Visions and Other Anomalous Phenomena among Participants in Candomblé, Umbanda, and Spiritism from Rio de Janeiro and Abadiania, Goias." Ph.D. Diss., University of California, Los Angeles.

Melville, Herman
1996 [1850]   "Hawthorne and His Mosses." In *The Piazza Tales and Other Prose Pieces, 1839–1860*. Vol. 9 of *The Writings of Herman Melville*, Edited by Harrison Hayford, Alma A. MacDougall, and G. Thomas Tanselle, 80. Evanston: Northwestern University Press.

Miller, Vincent J.
2004   *Consuming Religion: Christian Faith and Practice in a Consumer Culture*. New York: Continuum.

Morgan, David
1998   *Visual Piety: A History and Theory of Popular Religious Images*. Berkeley: University of California Press.

Murphy, Joseph M.
1988   *Santería: An African Religion in America*. Boston: Beacon Press.

Naipaul, V. S.
1980   *The Return of Eva Perón; with The Killings in Trinidad*. New York: Knopf.

Prida, Dolores
1991 [1985]   "Savings." In *Beautiful Señoritas and Other Plays*. Houston: Arte Publico Press.

Primiano, Leonard N.
1999   "Postmodern Sites of Catholic Sacred Materiality." In *Perspectives on American Religion and Culture*, edited by Peter W. Williams, 187–202. Malden, Mass: Blackwell Publishers.

Romberg, Raquel
2003   *Witchcraft and Welfare: Spiritual Capital and the Business of Magic in Modern Puerto Rico*. Austin: University of Texas Press.

Vélez, María Teresa
2000   *Drumming for the Gods: The Life and Times of Felipe García Villamil, Santero, Palero, and Abakuá*. Philadelphia: Temple University Press.

Wasson, R. G., et al.
1974   *Maria Sabina and Her Mazatec Mushroom Velada*. Ethnomycological Studies, no. 3. New York: Harcourt Brace Jovanovich.

Ybarra-Frausto, Tomas
1991   "*Rasquachismo:* A Chicano Sensibility." In CARA: *Chicano Art, Resistance, and Affirmation*, 155–62. Los Angeles: Wight Art Galley, University of California, Los Angeles.

SUGGESTED READINGS

GENERAL WORKS

Barnes, Sandra T.
1989   *Africa's Ogun.* Bloomington: Indiana University Press.

Cosentino, Donald J., ed.
1995   *Sacred Arts of Haitian Vodou.* Los Angeles: UCLA Fowler Museum of Cultural History.

Fernández Olmos, Margarite, and Lizabeth Paravisini-Gebert
2003   *Creole Religions of the Caribbean: An Introduction from Vodou and Santería to Obeah and Espiritismo.* New York: New York University Press.

Long, Carolyn Morrow
2001   *Spiritual Merchants: Religion, Magic, and Commerce.* Knoxville: University of Tennessee Press.

McDannell, Colleen
1995   *Material Christianity: Religion and Popular Culture in America.* New Haven: Yale University Press.

Thompson, Robert Farris
1993   *Face of the Gods: Art and Altars of Africa and the African Americas.* New York: Museum for African Art; Munich: Prestel.

AFRO-CUBAN RELIGIONS: SANTERÍA AND PALO

Aróstegui, Natalia Bolívar, and Carmen González Diaz de Villegas
1998   *Ta Makuende Yaya y Las Reglas de Palo Monte.* Havana: Ediciones Unión.

Barnet, Miguel
1996   "La Regla de Ocha: The Religious System of Santeria." In *Sacred Possessions: Vodou, Santeria, Obeah, and the Caribbean,* edited by Margarite Fernández Olmos and Lizabeth Paravisini-Gebert, 79–100. New Brunswick: Rutgers University Press.

Brandon, George
1993   *Santería from Africa to the New World: The Dead Sell Memories.* Bloomington: Indiana University Press.

Cabrera, Lydia
1986   *Reglas de Congo: Mayombe Palo Monte.* Miami: Ediciones Universal.

Flores-Peña, Ysamur, and Roberta J. Evanchuk
1994   *Santería Garments and Altars: Speaking without a Voice.* Jackson: University Press of Mississippi.

Izaguirre, Héctor
1998   *Palo Mayombé.* Caracas, Venezuela: Panapo.

Lindsay, Arturo, ed.
1996   *Santería Aesthetics in Contemporary Latin American Art.* Washington, D.C.: Smithsonian Institution Press.

Matibag, Eugenio
1996   *Afro-Cuban Religious Experience: Cultural Reflections in Narrative.* Gainesville: University Press of Florida.

Murphy, Joseph M.
1988   *Santería: African Spirits in America.* Boston: Beacon Press.

Wedel, Johan
2004   *Santeria Healing: A Journey into the Afro-Cuban World of Divinities, Spirits, and Sorcery.* Gainesville: University Press of Florida.

ESPIRITISMO

Harwood, Alan
1987   *Rx, Spiritist as Needed: A Study of a Puerto Rican Community Mental Health Resource.* Ithaca: Cornell University Press.

Garrison, Vivian
1977   "Doctor, *Espiritista*, or Psychiatrist?: Health-Seeking Behavior in a Puerto Rican Neighborhood of New York City." *Medical Anthropology* 1, no. 2: 65–180.

Morales, María Isabel
2001   "The José Movement: A New Phenomenon in Cuban Sprititualism." M.A. thesis, Florida International University.

Romberg, Raquel
2003   *Witchcraft and Welfare: Spiritual Capital and the Business of Magic in Modern Puerto Rico.* Austin: University of Texas Press.

CURANDERISMO

Gardner, Dore
1992   *Niño Fidencio: A Heart Thrown Open*. Photographs and interviews by Dore Gardner; essay by Kay Turner. Santa Fe: Museum of New Mexico Press.

Hudson, Wilson M., ed.
1951   *The Healer of Los Olmos and Other Mexican Lore*. Dallas: Southern Methodist University Press.

Kiev, Ari
1972   *Curanderismo: Mexican-American Folk Psychiatry*. New York: Free Press.

Roeder, Beatrice
1988   *Chicano Folk Medicine from Los Angeles, California*. Berkeley: University of California Press.

Sabina, María
2003   *Selections/María Sabina*. Edited by Jerome Rothenberg. Berkeley: University of California Press.

Trotter, Robert T., and Juan Antonio Chavira
1997   *Curanderismo: Mexican American Folk Healing*. 2nd ed. Athens: University of Georgia Press.

FOLK CATHOLICISM

Espín, Orlando
1997   *The Faith of the People: Theological Reflections on Popular Catholicism*. Maryknoll, N.Y.: Orbis Books.

Griffith, James S.
1987   "El Tiradito and Juan Soldado: Two Victim-Intercessors of the Western Borderlands." *International Folklore Review* 5: 75–81.

León, Luis D.
2004   *La Llorona's Children: Religion, Life, and Death in the U.S.-Mexican Borderlands*. Berkeley: University of California Press.

Matovina, Timothy, and Gary Riebe-Estrella, eds.
2002   *Horizons of the Sacred: Mexican Traditions in U.S. Catholicism*. Ithaca: Cornell University Press.

Pérez, Arturo, Consuelo Covarrubias, and Edward Foley, eds.
1994   *Así Es: Stories of Hispanic Spirituality*. Collegeville, Minn.: The Liturgical Press.

Pieper, Jim
2002   *Maximon/San Simon, Rey Pascual, Judas, Lucifer, and Others*. Los Angeles: Pieper and Associates.

Thompson, John
1994   "Santo Niño de Atocha." *Journal of the Southwest* (spring) 36, no. 1: 1–18.
1998   "Santisima Muerte: On the Origin and Development of a Mexican Occult Image." *Journal of the Southwest* (winter) 40, no. 4: 405–35.

INDEX